THE SECRET SAUCE

Presented by

Visionary Apostle Sabrina McKenzie

The Wealth Circle © 2023

ISBN: 979-8-218-22452-3

All rights reserved. No part of this publication may be reproduced, distributed, or transmitted in any form or by any means, including photocopying, recording, or other electronic or mechanical methods, without the prior written permission of the publisher, except in the case of brief quotations embodied in critical reviews and certain other noncommercial uses permitted by copyright law.

Table of Contents

Divine Laws of Business 1

When a Woman Forgives 31

Seeing Problems as Opportunities and Leveraging Them for Financial Gain 43

Goal Digger 52

It's a Lifestyle 63

Bizzie as a Bee for My Legacy 74

Mompreneur Making Passive Income with E-commerce 81

Wealth and Wellness is the Real Bag 88

Hype Vibes Recreational Self Care 96

Don't Get Out Hustled 102

How To Be a Lazy Entrepreneur 111

Self-Care 125

Mental Health - Think and Grow Rich 133

7 Steps to a 720 147

Divine Laws of Business

By Apostle Sabrina McKenzie

There are "Divine Laws Of Business" that guarantee your success!

The Dictionary states that a law is a system of rules which a particular country or community recognizes as regulating the actions of its members and which it may enforce by the imposition of penalties:

"They were taken to court for breaking the law", "law enforcement", "a license is required by law"

A law is a set of rules that are created and enforceable by social or governmental institutions to regulate behavior, with its precise definition a matter of longstanding debate.

There are Divine Laws on earth that are mandating your success, and these laws cannot be altered or changed by man, and once the statutes are followed, then you will succeed.

Therefore, laws are mandated and must be adhered to or there are penalties that must be paid. It is no different than the divine laws.

The "Divine Laws of Business" give us a license to do business and be blessed. It is a statute and a principle that God Himself follows and uses to bless all that follow the law.

God is not a respecter of persons but a respecter of His principle. That means God cannot lie. If you follow these principles then you will see your business scale. It's inevitable!

God is the divine code enforcer who will back you up; and who can change the plan of God? Follow the blueprint in the **"Divine Laws of Business"** and you are guaranteed to WIN.

The Divine Law of Business is not a prophecy but it's a principle just like natural and spiritual laws such as:

- sowing and reaping
- what goes up comes down
- what you do to others shall be done to you

It's a Divine LAW and THAT, God will not break.

Before you understand the Divine Laws of Business and get the knowledge you need to gain a new skill set or read anything in this book that will give you great depth, insight, and revelation on spiritual growth, self-care, investing, digital products, credit repair, and branding, you must first understand your PURPOSE.

That thing which is unique to only YOU.

What were you created to do?

Why were you born?

Why are you here?

Once you are clear on the intricate details that God is calling you to craft out on the earth, now it's GO TIME.

Let's Begin, What Is Your Purpose?

Your purpose is the direct reason God created you. Why were you placed on the earth?

What are you supposed to do with your life? How will you make a difference in the world?

These sound like loaded questions that would be difficult to answer. However, your purpose is easier to discover than you think. The great Myles Munroe said that If you want to find out how a Mercedes Benz works you don't' ask your local mechanic, but you take it to the Mercedes Benz manufacturer.

In order to understand what a product was created to do, you have to go to its creator.

Guess what? You are the product. In the same manner, to understand what you were created to do, it is necessary to go to your Creator. In Jeremiah 1:5, God tells Jeremiah, "Before I formed you in the womb, I knew you and before you were born, I consecrated you; I appointed you a prophet to the nations." Before Jeremiah was even conceived God had a purpose for his life. In the same manner, God has a purpose for your life, and He is more than happy to reveal that purpose to you. You must simply be willing to do the work.

Oftentimes if you have lived a life that has been filled with trouble, trauma, and tragedy, it can be difficult to imagine that God has anything good planned for your life. However, creating you for anything other than a good and grand purpose would go against both the word of God and His character. "For surely I know the plans I have for you", says the Lord, "plans for your welfare and not for harm, to give you a future with hope," reads Jeremiah 29:11.

Yes, the difficult things you have experienced in life may be overwhelming, but you must trust "that all things work together for good for those who love God, who are called according to His purpose". (Romans 8:28). As long as you are pursuing your purpose, God will use the bad, the complicated, and the hard times in your life for your good. God wants you to have an amazing life.

So even in the difficult times, you must remember that God does not end anything on a bad note.

As long as you continue on your journey, God will guide you to the good stuff. In other words, yet again, Romans 8:28, "All things are working together for the good of them that love the Lord and are called according to His purpose."

Identifying Your Purpose

Once you become acquainted with God and His identity for you, it is time to take the next steps toward identifying your purpose. When attempting to identify your purpose there are four questions you should ask yourself:

1) What did you want to do as a child?

2) What would you do for free?

3) What would you do if you knew you could not fail??

4) What does everyone come to you to do because you do it the BEST?

The answer to these four questions will help you determine what you naturally enjoy doing, which more than likely will be part of your purpose in some way or another. Additionally, your purpose will allow you to use your life experience and the lessons you learned during your journey to empower others. Your purpose is God's opportunity to use your inherent gifts, the things you are naturally good at doing for His glory. While your purpose will bring you great joy and fulfillment, it is important to remember that your purpose is not only about you. Your purpose will always be about the people you were placed on earth to serve. I liken one's purpose to an individual's fingerprint. Every individual walking the earth has fingerprints unique to them. A fingerprint provides you with the ability to leave your unique mark on whatever you touch, such as your purpose. God has given you a purpose unique to you. Your purpose is something that only you are able to perform.

Even if you are a doctor and there are thousands of other doctors in the world, there is uniqueness around the way that you practice medicine, that no one else possesses.

Because your purpose is uniquely specific to you, it is imperative that you discover the purpose for your life and walk in it daily. If you refuse to walk in your purpose, what happens to the individuals depending on the gifts and abilities God has given you to use?

The late and great Dr. Myles Munroe, President and Founder of Bahamas Faith Ministries International and Myles Munroe International, often spoke about people "taking the cure to the grave." You hold the solution to someone's problems in your hands, and when you refuse to discover and/or walk in your purpose, you are denying that person the solutions to their problems, solutions that God has specifically placed in you. What happens to those individuals who need what you have? You are a cure. You are an untapped answer. It is your responsibility to tap into this potential and share your gifts with the world.

At this moment, someone is desperately waiting for you to walk in your purpose and be their answer. Because of this, there is no time to make excuses for not being purpose driven. The timing to walk in your purpose will never be perfect. There will always be too little time, not enough money, and a million other things that require your immediate attention. Do not let this prevent you from walking in your purpose. If you could do this on your own, it would not be God's purpose for your life. God wants you to rely on Him as you walk in your purpose. He wants you to be dependent on Him. So do not look at your obstacles as stop signs or stumbling blocks. Look at them as opportunities for miracles and continue your journey of achieving purpose in your life. Boldly walk in the image of God and begin creating from nothing.

1. When something is a part of your purpose, you can keep doing it for countless hours. It's not like working on the clock, where you are counting down the hours and minutes; you ***actually enjoy it.***
2. Sometimes others will ask you to stop doing it because it can become obsessive; that's ***how much you enjoy it.***
3. If you were to fail at it, it would not matter because it makes you happy.

The Difference Between Those Who Fail and Those Who Succeed

Here are some commonalities of winners, those who are operating in their purpose. It's easier to follow these traits when you are doing something you love. The first step in purpose is **Not to Quit.** You must have resilience and be very passionate.

Don't quit. Statistics have proven that most businesses fail within the first five years and many of them quit once they fail. The difference between them and people who succeed is that winners **never, ever quit**. Losing is not an option.

Resilience: Thomas Edison

A reporter interviewed Thomas Edison and asked him if he felt like a failure and if he thought he should just give up by now. Edison replied, "Young man, why would I feel like a failure and why would I ever give up? I now know definitively over 9,000 ways that an electric light bulb will not work. Success is almost in my grasp."

After more than 10,000 attempts, Edison invented the light bulb.

Passion: Harland Sanders

Passion does not wait for the cards to be all lined up or for the situation to be favorable. It just continues to operate, creating a space for its creativity. Passion is the area that drives you when people say, "Are you still doing that? Isn't there an age requirement?"

They think that it makes no sense. It is the people who decide that, come hell or high water they are going to pursue their dreams that ultimately do attain their dreams.

Harland Sanders, who founded KFC, began selling fried chicken from his roadside restaurant in Corbin, Kentucky during the Great Depression. He did so well that he was the first person to start the restaurant franchising concept, with the first "Kentucky Fried Chicken" franchise opening in Utah in 1952.

Do you see what can happen even in the midst of a Great Depression? It does not matter if the economy is in a downward spiral, a decline, or a bailout. When you are operating from the abundance of your gifts you will be successful.

Myles Munroe said, "If you don't know the purpose of a gift, then abuse is inevitable." In essence, if you are doing something other than fulfilling your gift, then you are not releasing your full potential.

Now that you are clear about your purpose and direction, let's discuss the "Divine Laws of Business."

The Divine Laws of Business is the Understanding of Divine Laws. Here are some ideas that will help your business become a success. Remember, we are operating from the Divine Law, so what you do is as important as how you do it, and the reason why is that if you sow evil, you will reap evil. Below I've shared some helpful business principles that will cause the universe to favor you. It will attract high energy to you and allow the unseen to work on your behalf. Life nuggets that Divine Laws have taught me.

Believe It.

Understanding your purpose is one thing and I wish it was just as simple as that however, once you get purposeful, the enemy will try to take that purpose from you.

The enemy's job is to steal, kill, and destroy, so you have to fight for your purpose once you understand it. The great news is that the battle is not yours, it is the Lord's, so you can fight the good fight of faith. That means doing things religiously; that means being relentless, that means being faithful, that means being consistent, that means putting away childish things, and focusing fully on your faith, I want to give you some examples of what that looks like so that your faith may be strengthened.

You have to have a relentless attitude that no matter what comes, no matter who goes or through hell, or high water you're going to make it.

Just the other day I told someone that I won't take any more L's. You know, losses. The person said you will win or you will lose, but it's never a loss. I disagree with that philosophy. There is such a thing as losing.

I'm not the only one that has lost jobs, homes, cars, money, opportunities and more importantly family members but I got to a place where I said "Hell no, I'm done losing." We ain't losing nothing else and in fact, I'm in my season of recovery and that's when I saw my life shift in the direction of my thoughts. It's all in your mind. You have to condition your mind in the upward direction by any means necessary. The Bible says to be transformed by the renewing of your mind.

As a man thinks, so is he, and if you think I'm always taking L's or it's ok as long as it is a *lesson*, **then you will relive another lesson.**

Daggone it, I refuse to lose. I am from the school of thought that you either win or you win and with that in mind, I've never seen any great sportsman say "Oh I'm doing this and if it doesn't work, it's going to be a lesson." No. When Muhammad Ali used to fight in the boxing ring, I can remember him coming out saying "I am the greatest." He would say "You are a knucklehead if you get in this fight with me because I'm going to eat you alive. I'm going to send you back to your mother crying. I'm going to tear your head off. Nobody can compare to me because I am the greatest." Muhammad Ali would come out with such an assurance that if you were not confident in your own ability, then you would be very afraid.

This is the same confidence David had when he met Goliath and when everyone elsewas afraid. David said, "Who is this uncircumcised Philistine that dares to defile the army of our God?" Even if you're not a religious person, you can identify with 50 Cent's *Get Rich Or Die Trying*. Basically, they are all saying that they are not taking any L's and they are willing to fight until the end. Whoa! That's powerful. In fact, they all accomplished that goal. 50 Cent is rich and Muhammad Ali was the greatest.

That's the type of Godfidence that success requires.

God wants us to walk by FAITH. The Bible says that the just shall live by faith and without faith, it's impossible to please God.

If you are trying at anything you are failing, but you must do it and do it with the confidence that you will win!

Are you a Winner or Not?

Believe that the God that gave you the gift is able to fulfill the gift. You must have an undeniable faith that is an unshakable faith.

You must not have any type of doubt or residue of doubt, but believe that you are going to succeed by any means necessary. That means...

- You must be relentless
- You must believe that the greater one is inside of you and therefore you are the greatest
- Look, 50% of your battle is going to be the battle in your mind.
- To know That the God that gave you this idea is the same God that will complete

- To know that the God that gave you your purpose is the same God that will fulfill it and the same God that gave you this Destiny is going to see to it that you win.
- You Gotta know this and I mean you really gotta know it.
- Stop, sit, and just marinate in the fact that the God that gave you this purpose is more interested in fulfilling the purpose than you are in carrying the purpose out.

Once you really wrap your mind around that, you become like all of the other greats. You'll become like Michael Jordan who said, "Nobody is gonna beat me on the basketball court". You'll become like Tiger Woods who said, "Nobody can beat me in a golf game." You'll become like the greats who have preceded you. I cannot lose because I'm a WINNER!

People Pleasers

Do not let people transfer their doubt or fear on you. They will say things like, "No one has done that." No. YOU haven't done that!

They will say, "Are you sure you want to do that?" Yes, I'm positive. I am the greatest, in my Muhammad Ali voice, and I'm not going to let your inability to move by faith hinder my ability to trust God.

By Faith, I can do All things

By Faith, nothing is impossible to him that believes

By Faith, I can complete my assignment

By Faith, I will finish strong

Always remember that if you're trying you are failing. You must do it and SUCCEED.

Put it in Motion

When you understand that you're a winner because your God is a winner you will operate from that perspective. Put it in Motion!

People connect with people that have motion. Even the tides follow the current.

Tides are characterized by water moving up and down over a long period of time.

A tsunami is a series of extremely long waves caused by a large and sudden displacement of the ocean.

You have to put your vision in motion until it disrupts and shifts your current paradigm.

The force behind your continuous effort will break the dams and barriers in your life because EVERYTHING follows motion.

Once you understand that the GOD that you serve is the winner, therefore you are a winner, you have to put it in motion. People connect with you on social media because they see motion. Slow down on social media and watch your phone calls slow down. People and businesses connect with you because they see motion. You sent them a résumé and they liked the things that you said, therefore they call you. When sponsors and people that are looking at your content and your social media are following you, they are looking at your numbers. They are looking at your engagement. They follow people in motion. You have to put it in motion, you gotta create your constant, you gotta stay relevant on your pictures. Watch the people that are really excelling in the area of social engagement, which I called Global Integration. Those are people that have motion. You have to have Motion.

Let People Play Themselves

A lot of people will jump on your idea, but only five percent of the people will follow through. You have to let people play themselves out of your life. They are saying that they will help you but watch their actions and not their lip service. Let them play themselves. You can block, delete or mentally smile at them and give them no energy or time. Make no time for time wasters.

Roadblocks

People fear what they do not understand so you're always going to have a group of people talking about you because they don't understand your call.

News flash. Your call was not a conference call so they may never understand but you have to stay faithful to the call of God on your life. Ignore the haters. Ignore the slanderers. There will be 2 types of people that don't understand you.

The first person is the person that literally just doesn't get it but they want to understand so they can help you.

The second person is dangerous because they are assigned to you by the enemy to destroy you. They are the people that will come and see your vision and talk behind your back and steal your ideas all the while diminishing your vision or gift.

They will come into your vision and formulate groups inside the vision to create division. Be sure to stay clear of those people, and as my grandmother would say feed them with the long-handled spoon.

Don't give them any pertinent information. Don't give them any details because what they're really trying to do is copy you. Rest assured that the great thing about those that copy you is that they are really in awe of your gift. Copying is the best form of flattery.

You need to remember, "By the time you copy me I'm already doing something different." People that have to copy you and emulate you do this because they have not spent enough time in God's presence to get their own revelation.

Typically people that copy are not innovators nor inventors and they have to keep looking at other people to get ideas. Don't worry about these small-minded people because they will eventually be cut off. I said it. "Cut them Off!" When a doctor finds a cancerous cell in the body he does not say. "Oh let me ignore this and it will go away." No. He says, "Let me try radiation, chemotherapy, or anything that will burn and drive the cancer out." because he understands that it will metastasize and grow.

When you let negative people sit in your vision, you will pay the price of them infecting the body. Cut them off!

Don't worry about the haters, they'll fall off, don't worry about the copiers, if they had your shoes they still couldn't walk in them, and don't worry about the envious. Your goal is to make sure that you're not one of them.

Now it's time to Go!

Go! In spite of your fear.

Go! In spite of your failure.

Go! In spite of your flaws.

Go! In spite of your haters.

Go! Go! Go!

Divine Law Number 1. Use no Deception.

Use no Deception. We must always be truthful, both inside the company and to our customers and we must never use deception for gain or any other reasons.

Divine Law Number 2. Make The Best Quality Product.

Make certain that all products and actions are beneficial and operate with excellence in community service. Everything done must have an overall beneficial effect. Steve Jobs said, "My best contribution is not settling for anything but really good stuff. Our goal is to make the best devices in the world, not to be the biggest."

Divine Law Number 3. You Must Have Faith.

Faith. We will trust God! Faith is the evidence of God in the things unseen. You must believe that God has the power to do the impossible through you and if not you, then who else? Faith keeps you going when everything else around you is falling apart. How do you know that you have faith?

Faith is a verb, it is a physical demonstration of what you are believing God to do.

Example: If you want to write a book, but you don't have money or a distribution deal and you don't know how to organize your thoughts. **Faith Must Take Action.**

Example: You can organize your thoughts then go to Google and look at YouTube videos of how other people do it. Seek mentors, write a chapter every week, create an outline, and get a graphic artist to design the cover.

Faith Takes Action! Become an ACTIONAIRE. This is a colloquialism coined by one of the first black billionaires, Michael Roberts.

Divine Law Number 4. Strive to Have The Best Environment.

We shall strive to have the best environment. We shall do our best to maintain a spirit of diligence, faithfulness, excellence, trust, peace, and harmony that shall transcend the office and spread to our personal relationships.

Divine Law Number 5. We Constantly Improve.

We must constantly improve. Each day, each week, each month, each quarter, each year, and each decade, we shall strive to be better than we were before. If you can't, spend an hour in prayer, reading a book, or in the gym. Take 10 minutes each day, but ALWAYS improve.

Divine Law Number 6. Giving Back Your Time and Talents.

Giving. As we are blessed, we shall bless others. Russell Simmons said in his book "Do You," Give yourself, content, and your products away until they can't live without you."

Divine Law Number 7. Niche Your Way To The Top!

Don't dissipate your energies on the sidelines. Find your niche and understand your niche. I am a dancer; however, I fall in the company of thousands of other dancers who have probably taken ballet since they were three years old. If I were to compete with them, I would be lost in a pool of great dancers. However, I knew my niche was connected to spiritual dance. My desire to worship God is just as intense as my desire to dance. They were one and the same because I use my dance as a form of worship, it made perfect sense to me to be the Dancing Preacher! Branding myself as the Dancing Preacher, enabled me to meet the needs of a specific group of individuals who are liturgical dancers. Very quickly I became an expert in the field because there were not many people who specialized in that area. An expert requires having a background in theology as well as training in dance.

Your niche is going to set you a cut above the rest. There are some pros and cons, but your positive advantages will outweigh the bad.

The Pros of Niche Marketing

With niche marketing, you have an instant target audience that adores your brand. Why?

Because they are generally doing the same thing as you are. It helps them to easily identify with you. One of the greatest keys of marketing is the idea of brand identity. People don't want to just buy a product; they want to feel like the product represents who they are and what they believe. You find a greater sense of loyalty to brands that identify with groups.

Divine Law Number 8. Teamwork Makes the Dream Work.

People that are competing are at the bottom because the winners are to busy collaborating at the TOP! See you at the Top.

The book that you are reading right now is the direct result of collaboration. I'm not only sharing my success, but you are hearing from others who are also successful. There is not one person that can be great at everything. But when you work with a team, you actually improve your value at a quicker rate. It's called organized effort! Mastermind is a score of minds where no one person is the mastermind in the spirit of harmonious cooperation. I believe God designed it that way; the Body of Christ is made up of many gifts called the five-fold ministry and each gift works together to benefit the others. I am sure that if one person had all of the gifts, he/she would probably not share or work with anyone. That's why, according to the five-fold ministry, we must work together. (Ephesian 4:12)

Combined power, material and moral advantages, churches, schools, and the news media modify the business ethic that it would be suicide for anyone to come against them. Power is an organized effort. The accumulation of great wealth is based on the ability to comprehend and execute knowledge and psychology.

Now I dare you to try these Divine Laws of Business and watch your business take off like a space ship all the way to the top, no, better yet, all the way to the bank.

You must also remember that there are other facets to your road to success as you will see in the following pages of this book.

You must walk in forgiveness; You should learn to see problems as opportunities and leverage them for financial gain. Your client communication must be excellent and provide a template for the legacy of your business. You must pivot and use your creativity in the marketplace realizing that wealth and wellness, self-care, and balance are key to your sustaining and growing your business.

You should also learn the lesson of always working harder than the next person while having a wealth mindset and yes, taking care of your credit.

You are the product and God will use you as a template and benchmark for others.

Divine Laws of Business

Apostle Sabrina McKenzie

Connect with Apostle Dr. Sabrina McKenzie

Websites:

www.Sabrinamckenzie.org

www.Wealthcircle.us

Instagram @Pastorsabrinamk

Facebook @DrSabrinaMckrnzie

Meet

Apostle Sabrina McKenzie is a Women's Rights Activist, Celebrated Pastor, Businesswoman, and Television

Personality on Bravos "In A Mans World:' Affectionately known as "The Dancing Preacher",

McKenzie is the founder and the Executive Producer of Dancing Preachers International and the Founder of Liturgical Dance Day. She is best known for her role in creating one of the most celebrated liturgical dance ministries, the International Dance Commission (IDC), which has gained international acclaim since its inception in 2005. Under her leadership, the organization has grown from 40 members to over 2,780 members worldwide, which includes 40 chapters.

A trailblazer in her own right, Women's Activist and Mentor to thousands of Women

- Co-authored Equal Rights Amendment Bill 2018 in the Georgia House Of Representatives
- Co-authored Prayer In School Bill 2015 in the Georgia House Of Representatives
- Founder of The Legislative Clergy Council
- Founder of the National Taskforce Against Domestic Violence

- Founder of Epic Women Leadership
- Founder of Celebrities Against Domestic Violence
- Founder of Dancing Preachers International
- Founder of Liturgical Dance Day
- Founder of the International Dance Commission
- Author of 11 Books
- Ordained Apostle
- Certified Chaplain CPE Emory Hospital
- Bravo TV "In A Mans World"

Through her countless efforts to be a driving force of change, McKenzie has been featured in national media platforms such as CNN, Essence, The New York Times, NBC, Rolling Out, Fox, CBS Atlanta, and more.

Message to the Reader:

On the following pages are testimonies of women who have persevered through the storms of life to come out victorious on the other side. These women bare their souls on their journey to success and in the midst of telling their story, they share their "secret sauce" to wholeness and entrepreneurship.

We hope that you will enjoy these diverse anecdotes from all walks of life and that you will be blessed in the process.

Min. Kimberly A. Clemons Presents…

When a Woman Forgives

I was inspired to start my business after God healed me from the hurt and pain that I carried for many many years. Because I was raped from ages 5-14, and could not speak up about it until I was 35 years old, I had hit the lowest of the lowest in my life. I hated myself, and the entire world and at one time thought it would be best to escape and be free from this world. I always thought: Why didn't anyone help me? Why did that happen to me? I thought I was the only one in the whole world going through it. As an adult, I became fearful of everything. Bitterness, hatred, and anger ruled my life. For many years, my life spiraled downward as I recalled, replayed, and believed those threats and negative words which had haunted me since my childhood. What was said to me repeatedly for years, unfortunately, I began to believe those words whispered to me in a forceful tone; "No one will ever, ever want you"! "No one will ever, ever believe you"! "You will never be nothing"! I could not help but hate myself. I blamed myself for many years for not speaking up.

The day I decided to confront the person who had ruined my childhood was the day that I came face to face with my greatest fear of not being believed. Yes, he not only denied it; but he called me a liar and told other people we knew that I was lying. Sadly, he convinced them to be on his side. I felt alone, confused, rejected and I was fueled with rage. During my rage, I cried out to God and asked the best question I had at that moment. I asked God; What kind of God are you that YOU would allow a child to be raped?

That was the turning point of my life with hearing from God. I learned that God hears, and He answers! God said "I am the kind of God that allowed you not to get pregnant. I am the kind of God that kept you from sexually abusing anyone, I am the kind of God that did not allow you to get addicted to drugs, and I am the kind of God that kept you from losing your mind. I am the kind of God that…" Each time I heard God tell me what kind of God He is, I became weaker and weaker. I decided to surrender my will and let God into my life, and He showed me that although I went through that trauma, He was with me. He protected me from so much and He would use that evil for good.

God allowed me to cross paths with two women (Lady Angela Cadwell and Minister Sharon Roberts) who helped me tremendously in my life to heal, forgive, love, and embrace peace. I started The Girls Factory because I heard God say, *"Help the young girls."* My purpose and passion are undeniably from God for His children. I have an unexplainable deep desire to encourage and empower young girls. I'm committed to bringing awareness to domestic violence issues and sexual traumas as I empower girls to stay safe and persevere through their challenges. It is important for me to promote forgiveness while encouraging girls to know who God says they are, and to confidently care about themselves so they will choose not to repeat the negative generational and societal cycles they may be exposed to. God sends the girls to me. So many moms, dads, grandparents, siblings, and teachers ask me to help their girls, especially when the girls have challenging attitudes and behavioral issues. My daily prayer is, "Use me God! Send me God, and I will go!" I will go wherever God wants me to go. I just want to do His will for my life.

The Girls Factory is all about building girls to be confident, courageous, compassionate, creative, and culturally aware despite the traumas they may encounter. I provide a safe space for young girls to talk about their triumphs and challenges. The girls learn life skills through coaching and cooking. I offer Listening Sessions, Cooking Sessions, Workshops, and Community Engagement. The workshops I provide include the girls taking home fun gifts that will help them to put what they learn into practice.

What makes The Girls Factory unique and sets us apart from competitors is that we encourage and empower girls to be who they are created to be. We give them the space to share what's on their hearts and help them to be aware of the challenges girls may face and provide positive solutions to help them as they journey to womanhood. The Girls Factory is not afraid to talk about issues that affect girls. We partner with positive women in the community, including the senior community, and those who love to cook and share recipes. We share "Girl Talk" with no judgment zones. We host an annual Tea Party, Rites of Passage, and Purity Ball Event. The girls learn the importance of respect, forgiveness, and honor, and they are afforded opportunities to display the Fruit of the Spirit. The Girls Factory loves to give and the girls strive in excellence to grow to become cheerful givers while serving others in need.

There are of course challenges that I have faced as a business owner. My challenges were having a stony heart and not knowing who God called me to be. I simply did not believe God knew what He was doing. I chose to believe the negative words that were imparted to me as a child. God told me to start my organization and because of fear, doubt, and confusion, I started, but then stopped doing what God gave me to do and decided to serve with another girls program. For years, it was easy to run and hide because I was afraid of failing and afraid of what others would think of me doing what God said. God never stopped chasing me. While on the run, I believe I heard from God, "That is nice that you are serving and helping this organization, but I gave you something to do, KIMBERLY!"

Although I was fearful to let go of serving with the other organization, I decided to listen to God. I squared my shoulders and let it go. It was not easy. My heart felt bad and it felt like I was abandoning the organization and the girls. God showed me by being obedient, He would take care of me and guide me every step of the way. I was blessed tremendously going into schools, homes, churches, and community centers to give girls what God gave me to give to them. I am no longer bound by negative talk from myself or bound by what people think I should or should not be doing. I trust God with everything in me and when I get weak, God reminds me of who He is and has been in my life. I know without a doubt, obedience is better than sacrifice.

My biggest success has been learning about my purpose, believing God's purpose for my life and being able to receive God's forgiveness while truly forgiving others. Also, trusting God and watching God open doors for me to serve young girls and women around the world. Knowing that I can share my testimony to help girls and women overcome is another success for me. Honestly, another one of my biggest successes is being able to discern God in every aspect of my life, letting go of bitterness, hatred, unforgiveness, and pride. Being free from fear and choosing to love and forgive is priceless.

The best way for me to stay motivated and focused on my goals is to pray, watch and listen for God to show me the way. I speak the Word and take captive those negative thoughts when they come to me. I will never forget where God brought me from, and I get energized to serve God and His children even more. Knowing that I am able to encourage the girls and give them the tools that I did not have is so rewarding. I learned to not compare myself to others -- just be me and appreciate who I am and what God has given me. I believe in the promises of God. I share my concerns with God and with positive people. I write things down and journal often to remember to be grateful for it all.

In 5 or 10 years, I envision The Girls Factory to be a global resource and outlet for girls. I see myself traveling around the world listening and speaking with young girls ages 8-17 yrs., helping them to understand that they are not alone, they have a voice, they are beautiful, and they are valuable.

Here is what I would advise others to do if they are considering the entrepreneurial Journey. Ask God who you are and what you are purposed to do. Trust God and believe that you can be who He says you are and you can choose to do His will. Be obedient and authentic. Do not compromise your morals and values. Do not be afraid to ask for help. Take classes and put what you learn into practice. Do not procrastinate. Do not doubt. Do not worry. Research and obtain as much information as you can about your business and your competitors. Do not allow fear to stop you from moving forward. Everyone will not understand your journey as you strive to grow and be successful in business; do not get discouraged when people share their opinions and thoughts about what they think you should or should not do. Stay focused and continue to take time for yourself to clearly hear from God. Do not be afraid to fail. Search your heart and remember your why. Do not be jealous or envious of others, especially those who are excelling or prospering faster than you. Never bad mouth or gossip about your competitors. Put God first, and speak life over yourself and your business.

It is important to have core values that guide your business and influence your decision-making and interactions with customers and employees. To stay true to these core values I remind myself daily to:

- Be honest with myself and have excellent integrity.
- Know what kind of a person I am and strive to be better in every aspect of my life.
- Be a woman with good character and build positive relationships while learning when to move on.
- Be sure to look for God, recognize what God is saying, seek godly counsel, wisdom, and choose to stand firm in my own decision.
- Be responsible and accountable for my own actions.
- Do not judge others and diligently pray for them and do what I can to provide help but do not be a hindrance in their life.
- Know that God is my standard.
- Treat others the way that I want to be treated.
- Take care of my mind, body, and spirit.

- Know that it is important for me to love myself and treat myself with love, respect, kindness, compassion, and understanding.
- Know who I am and be who I am and never covet what someone else has.

If you are in business, let me encourage you to:

- Put God first and give Him all the Glory.
- Seek his righteousness.
- Put your faith and trust in God, not in man.
- Be anxious for nothing.
- Search your heart; release any hurt, bitterness, worry, doubt, procrastination, envy, carnality, or unforgiveness, and ask the Holy Spirit to show you yourself.
- When it gets rough, surrender to God's will, remember the word that you have hidden in your heart, and you will get through it.
- Only take responsibility for your own actions. Remember the battle is not yours and there is a spiritual war that is constantly happening.
- Everything you need is inside of you, believe and choose to be positive.

- Know that God is with you. If He told you to do it, He is with you every step of the way and He will provide for your every need.
- You cannot serve two masters, when you make a choice on whom you will serve, accept the consequences and outcomes of your choice.
- Never give up, never compromise, and never allow anyone to steal your joy.
- Know that you were created for a purpose and your life is not your own.
- Seek truth and reject the lies that will come from you and to you.
- When you make mistakes, learn from them and do not condemn yourself; forgive yourself and forgive others daily.
- Be careful of your thoughts, be kind to yourself, and treat yourself with the utmost respect.
- Take yourself seriously and have fun because you only get one life to live.
- You deserve the best! Know the Truth, Believe the Truth, and Live Truth!
- Know that you are loved and your life is worth living no matter what you have been through!

- There is nothing too hard for God and know that He sees you, He hears you, He knows you better than you know yourself so Give God a try.
- Do not be afraid and when you become afraid, confess it and receive the Peace that the Holy Spirit will give you that is everlasting!
- Be the Light if you find yourself in a dark place or around dark people. Never give in or give up!

Now go forth giving thanks and being grateful for all that God has for you!

When a Woman Forgives

Connect with Min. Kimberly Clemons

- www.iamthegirlsfactory.org
- kimberlyclemons1998@gmail.com
- Kimberly Stanton Clemons (Facebook)
- iamkimberly_clemons (IG)

Meet Min. Kimberly A. Clemons

Min. Kimberly A. Clemons is a loving, kind, compassionate, giving, and forgiving Spirit. She builds up girls to be confident, courageous, compassionate, creative, and culturally aware. She is a Wife, Mother, Minister/Chaplain, Founder of The Girls Factory, Author, Life Coach, and Entrepreneur. Min. Clemons has a bachelor's from Grace College Theological & Seminary, becoming a Licensed and Ordained Minister, serving youth in the church and the community, advocating for youth and survivors of domestic violence and sexual abuse, being a published author (*Overcome Fear Knots, Prayer Untangles, So…. Fear Not*), serving with the Detroit Police Department Chaplain (DPDCC), being an international speaker. She believes that every girl should know how special they are, and they should have an outlet to speak up and out against issues that bring them harm.

Seeing Problems as Opportunities and Leveraging Them for Financial Gain

By Tera Carissa Hodges

Though I have worked public relations and marketing side gigs such as conferences, trade shows, etc. since moving to Atlanta in 2006, after graduating from undergrad in 2005, in conjunction with my 9 to 5, in 2010 I launched Life Now Coaching, now LR (Life Redefined) International in partnership with my ministry and speaking endeavors. So often after ministering, women wanted more. This inspired me to launch my coaching practice in an effort to further teach and connect. Through my coaching endeavors, I identified how most women I coached were in pain and felt stuck. But, by helping them identify their purpose, they achieved healing and empowerment taking place and in some cases, making them rich. So I began helping women identify their pain, search for the purpose for it, and create a business, mentorship program, or product from it. I just believe pain should make you rich!

From there, in 2016, I decided that not only did women need this, but I revisited my corporate roots to help businesses, ministries, brands, and personalities that have weathered storms and could benefit just the same. This is the foundation of LR (Life, Labels, Lifestyles) Redefined International.

LR is all about being empowered, despite circumstances and rebounding after a storm. We all go through obstacles, but it is our choice to grow through obstacles and turn the obstacles into opportunities that work for us.

Either through LR International directly or through business partnerships, I currently offer personal coaching, business coaching, apparel, PR/media services, empowerment greeting cards, product development, empowerment classes, and more…and we are still growing. Past clients have had their products featured in Vogue, Walmart, national television, and so on. My apparel has been worn and endorsed by celebrities: Amara La Negra, Porsha Williams, Cece Winans, and others.

While my business is mainstream, it is also unique and set apart from competitors because I am proudly faith-based. Clients are used to me saying, let me pray about it. While making money is a goal, it is not the bottom line. The bottom line is peace, purpose, empowerment, and personal fulfillment. Each product and or service is designed for the recipient to walk away empowered. That is the goal.

Though my business is faith and empowerment-based, does that mean everything has been roses? Of course not! Considering some of the challenges I have faced as a business owner, I realized that you will always have copycats. I overcome them by continuing to be myself and doing things in alignment with my purpose to empower others. That is what sets me apart. Usually, copycats jump from one person to another to gain ideas to mimic. Eventually, because they are driven by what they believe is working or selling in the moment, they will find another identity to duplicate and move on. And any business they garnered while copying me will inevitably come to me because the people truly looking for that service, etc., still have a need the copycat is no longer fulfilling. So I would say perseverance and commitment to who I really am is how I have overcome them. Additionally, staying focused on my lane has blessed me tremendously. Horses don't win races looking to the left or the right. They win them by focusing forward.

Finally, anger is an obstacle I have had to overcome. When you are winning, there will be people who don't like your wins, who will want to tear down everything they see you doing out of anger and jealousy. But there are remedies for that too! I discuss this and offer resources on www.successbullying.us

While obstacles have come, so have victories. My biggest success so far has been making a million by the age of 35. It has been my greatest achievement financially thus far. I achieved that primarily through coaching. I used to do one-on-one coaching sessions when I first started in 2010. With hundreds of thousands of supporters, I can rarely, if ever, offer one-on-one's and certainly not at the price point I offered in the beginning. So group coaching, group empowerment calls, my 1K subscribers (1,000+ people who participate in my subscription service and receive empowerment messages throughout the week) got me there. People, especially women, are willing to invest in themselves at an affordable amount to be inspired, empowered, and get the information they need to produce better life results. That is the market I am tapped into.

Being affordable is also part of that million-dollar formula. Yes, there are coaching options out there for thousands of dollars. And yes, I have some of those. Once I have coached you personally or if you are a business owner whose business can sustain it, I have offers that go up to $10,000. But, as I teach my clients who have customers, to win financially, you have to have something for everybody. How that translates for me is you can get empowerment from me for $20 a month through my subscription service which you can find information for at www.teracarissa.com 1KSubscribers, or a customized one for thousands. Millions are found in providing multiple options. While empowering others and reaping the financial harvest from that is rewarding, what keeps me motivated is focusing on how I can win in all aspects of my life.

In order to stay motivated and focused on my goals, my strategies include prayer, eating healthy, working out, and enjoying life. These are excellent motivators that help me stay focused on my goals, the things that matter, and my bottom line. I think people discount how eating healthy, taking vitamins, and exercising can impact your mood. I think people forget the power of prayer. I certainly believe people don't realize how much nature can calm you, empower you, and inspire you. It's why I travel as often as I do. It is enjoyable and inspiring. I was just reading an article today about how just seeing water for 20 minutes can shift your mood positively. So, if you don't live near water, if you can, take a trip there. Maybe you can't go to a 5-star beach resort, but how about a nearby lake? Start somewhere. Mountains are inspiring too. Being able to treat myself to enjoy these things are excellent motivators to keep going, keep inspiring, and empowering other people while also preparing for the victories I am anticipating ahead.

My vision for the future of my business 5 to 10 years from now is to have launched multiple products and services for parents and the businesses that serve them. My vision is to remain faith-based and influence others to integrate into the mainstream to be a beacon of hope, light, and empowerment that positively impacts the masses.

Likewise, I would tell anyone that if you are considering the entrepreneurial journey, you must first know the reason why.

So often I coach people who are inspired to get started because they like what they see someone else doing, but that is not enough. That is not a firm enough foundation to build anything. You have to have a WHY for yourself, a purpose. That is what will keep you going when obstacles arise when people begin to hate you for your success, when the wrong life partner is drawn to you because of your success and only wants a piece of your success. Trying to duplicate someone else won't produce enough willpower to maintain through a storm. So knowing your why is the first thing every entrepreneur needs to get crystal clear on.

This is why, for me, every product, business, or service must have a bottom-line commitment to positively impact others. This core value guides my business and influences my decision-making and interactions with customers as well as employees. Positivity is the vision that guides me.

I encourage every entrepreneur to have a vision for your business and who you are as the CEO/Founder of that business and strive towards that daily.

Furthermore, do not wait until things are perfect to get started. Perfection is at the finish line, not the starting line. You grow as you go. Start off as professionally as possible and get better with time. Remember, the Amazon we know today is not the Amazon it was when it first got started; neither are Coca-Cola, Google, and other companies. Everything grows as it goes. Also, keep in mind failure is not defeat. Failure is an opportunity to learn. McDonald's has launched products only to pull them off their menu later. Walmart has launched products only to stop production later. Such is business and that's ok. But you won't know this if you don't surround yourself with other positive, productive, ever-evolving entrepreneurs. This is why networking is key and community matters. No one is meant to do it alone. Join that business league, seek out multiple mentors, and read books on the topic you are seeking to be successful in. That's how you win. That's how you keep going.

Seeing Problems as Opportunities and Leveraging Them for Financial Gain.

Connect with Tera Carissa Hodges:

- www.teracarissa.com
- tera@teracarissa.com

Meet Tera Carissa Hodges

Tera Carissa Hodges is an entrepreneur, author, speaker, and coach that empowers women to tap into their life experiences to build purpose-based businesses, and thrive economically, and personally.

Tera has been featured in several magazines such as Forbes, Essence Magazine, Black Enterprise, and as the headliner at a Mercedes Benz-sponsored Women's Conference in Johannesburg, South Africa for her expertise.

She has coached an estimated 10,000 women in over 30 countries. Tera is motivated by Seeing positive women win against all odds and live in their purpose. Be on the lookout for her future endeavors; she will be developing tools and resources for healthy parenting.

Goal Digger

By Santanna Lively

While watching the struggle within my family. I never imagined growing up that I'd be in business for myself. I was taught in my home to get a good-paying job and seek the American Dream. In my community, a good-paying job was ideally a plant manufacturing job. Detroit is known for its Big 3: Chrysler, Ford, and GM. We didn't entertain many options to be more. I, on the other hand, wanted to be a defense attorney. I was my mom's most outspoken child and the one that talked way too much for my own good. Watching my mother struggle to provide for all seven of us, even having the help of my grandparents, was enough to inspire me to be great in whatever it was I chose to do.

As I grew older, my passion to become an attorney never changed until, of course, I discovered the world of finance. My very first business wasn't even a business. It was more like a hustle. I didn't have the knowledge at the time to register a business, obtain a Tax ID number and actually make it legit, so I did credit repair and taxes from my home. I got started following the discharge of every 9-5 job I had. I either got burnt out on the assignments or they were eager to change their managerial styles, which always resulted in termination. Needless to say, I needed to work for myself. I started by using myself as my very first client. I prepared my own taxes, and I repaired my own credit.

Learning Credit Repair was tons of trial and error along with studying and staying abreast of consumer law. The most exciting thing about that is the fact that I still had an opportunity to do what I dreamed of doing as a kid. Also, I'd be able to help people out of problematic circumstances. I created methods that were easy for me to achieve and practiced repetitiveness until I mastered my craft.

I realized that some time had gone by, and I hadn't had a job in a while. That gave me all the confidence I needed to feel secure in the position I'd created for myself. Shortly after, I obtained an office space and legitimized my business. I got my articles of organization, Tax ID Number, phone number, and email address. I was proud to announce the birth of Excellent Choice Financial on October 29, 2015. It started off rocky and at times; I only made enough to pay my bills. Other times, I barely broke even. I realized that what I needed was consistency and structure. That is when I converted my once hustle into a real business.

Excellent Choice Financial eventually became a financial one-stop shop. I offered credit repair, entity structure, grant writing, tax preparation, business plans, and employment resource assistance. I became a magnet for people who desired some assistance with bettering their lives. I can't even count how many people I've helped who have thanked me over the years for the services I've provided. My clients and I created long-term bonds that resulted in them being in my life for many years. Whenever they needed anything, they'd always come back to me. Later, I added a few other services to my roster and branched into other arenas. Real estate came naturally and so did business credit and funding. During the pandemic, I took that time to get back in school and certify myself for the additional services. I became a real estate broker and opened my brokerage, Ritzy Realty.

My business is unique because of the love and passion I have for my clients. This sets me aside from some other businesses. I actually love what I do, and I enjoy seeing the satisfaction I bring people. I'm in the business of bettering others and it makes me feel good to watch them grow. I'm the silent cheerleader that stands beside my clients during their journey to success. I discovered my calling when I got into this line of work. There has never been a time where I was unable to assist someone coming to me for the services I offer. To be honest, my clients are the ones that created the extended services I've added to my roster. They know to contact me first regarding anything, and if I can't do it, I'll learn how to just for them. I take extreme pleasure in being that "Go to Gal."

As all business owners know, there will be challenges. One of the biggest challenges I've faced was consistency. There have been countless times in business when I just wanted to throw in the towel because business was slow. As a matter of fact, I have taken breaks and even ventured into other areas, but always came right back. I wondered if it was personal or if the services I offered were not as essential as I viewed them to be. However, my solution was to keep at it. Most people starting fresh in business for themselves expect their consumers to be their family and friends. Well, think again! If you only market to people you know, your business will have a very short run. I discovered that it isn't the ones you know that'll support you to the extremity, it's the ones you don't know that you will impact the most. I also realized that consumers like convenience. I had to get out of the mindset of running a traditional business and accept the latest business trends.

In thinking about my successes, I've had many throughout the journey of my career.

However, my greatest accomplishment was the opening of my real estate brokerage "Ritzy Realty." I opened my brokerage during a very dark time in my life. Not only was I having personal issues, but I also sat back along with the entire world watching millions die from COVID. I lost very close friends and relatives, with one being my grandmother. I didn't know if this would be the end of time for mankind or if it was indeed a conspiracy. All I knew was that everything I wanted to achieve, I was determined to fulfill. Ritzy Realty seemed unreachable. My husband coached me to broaden my horizon of positive thinking and helped me overcome the doubts I had. He made me create bigger visions and set goals that seemed unachievable just to push me to work harder.

I've never admitted this to anyone else, but this was the first business that gave me internal excitement. When I saw the finished product, Ritzy Realty signs and logos everywhere, and an office filled with "Ritzy" merch, I cried and broke down to my knees thanking God for this business. It seemed so far out of reach for me to achieve, but I did it. Doubt filled my mind and negativity set in, but I was not defeated. I got licensed, built my brand, and opened those doors.

I stay motivated by knowing I am an example. My daughter watches me and has picked up on many of my ways. She keeps me motivated and focused on succeeding. I want to create a legacy that will be carried on for generations. I understand the importance of setting a solid foundation for my offspring and I plan to stand on it. At the age of 12, my daughter understands the concept of essential life. She knows what life's necessities consist of, and I stress to her the importance of hard work. I am encouraged to be better at everything I do to assure a promising future for her. I'm not aiming to make things easy for her, but I don't want her to face the barriers I endured trying to find my way in life. I love this quote by Theodore Roosevelt: "Nothing worth having comes easy," and through experience, I am teaching her this. I teach her the things I know, and I make her work for what she wants.

When I see my business in the future, I envision Ritzy Realty becoming a popular franchise throughout the entire US. I want to employ agents that are adamant about creating their own destinies. I want my brokerage to become that life-changing opportunity for buyers, sellers, investors, and agents. My goal is to start by opening a brokerage in the major cities of America and documenting our growth via reality TV. This journey needs to be televised because it's not often that any positive light is shown on successful women in business from Detroit. I plan to see Ritzy Realty on the NYSE (New York Stock Exchange and Nasdaq) and be responsible for new construction and affordable housing in developing cities. Within the next 10 years, Ritzy Realty will be the most prominent pipeline for all real estate transactions and development, both residential and commercial.

In this as well as other businesses, you must remember innovation and creativity. With the way of life and business trends changing so rapidly, the best way to stay up to date is to read. Reading has enabled me to advance my business to accommodate technology, trends, and conveniences. This is one of the most important tools I've found necessary to stay in business. I mentioned earlier how people love convenience these days but in addition, they love technology. I plan to implement virtual real estate for those in the Metaverse. With the upcoming expansion of digital currency, virtual assets will give its users a feeling of ownership and investment opportunity. This is an implementation that not everyone is happy about because it looks and feels unreal, but I'd be the first to say that it is time to officially embrace the way of the world.

As a business owner, I have some values that I adhere to, no matter what. My core value is integrity. Being in a business where I am responsible for handling such delicate information, trust and honesty is very important. I take pride in offering that to my clients, as they've been receptive to it for as long as I've been in business. Lasting relationships and even some friendships have stemmed from my integrity in business. I make sure my clients' files are always safe and secure and treat them just as I would my very own. I love the trust that my clients have in me, and I would never do anything to jeopardize that. Bringing aboard other members to my team becomes a very critical task for me. I have to make sure that not only are the applicants a good fit for my company, but also a good fit for my clients. I can only employ trustworthy, honest people to work in the field I'm in due to the delicacy of my client's data.

To measure success you must keep track of your goals. My success is measured in terms of growth. I base my progress on where I am and what I have today as opposed to yesterday, this year opposed to last year, and so forth. So far, I have been lucky to add to my totem pole each year. As real estate investors, my husband and I are building our portfolio of homes by purchasing 1-2 homes each year. We've been successful at it thus far and plan to double that quota very soon. One way I encourage you all to stay ahead of yourself is to write out your goals and deadlines. It's one thing to have desires, but writing them out creates visions. I love speaking to audiences regarding growth and elevation because I teach against stagnancy. Even when the growth is minimal, it is recognizable and offers self-gratification and motivation to keep pushing. Another important thing to remember is "Time." Time is something we don't get back. Don't waste time doing anything you can't imagine doing forever.

"You'll Never Get The Chance To Relive Yesterday, But You'll Always Have Time To Prepare For Tomorrow"

-Santanna Lively

Goal Digger

Santanna Lively

Connect with Santanna Lively

Real Estate Broker

Ritzy Realty

25900 Greenfield Rd Ste 350

Oak Park, MI 48237

(313) 229-6215

Meet Santanna Lively

Santanna Lively is the "Queen of Fix and Flips." If you ever desire to discuss money, she's always available to "Talk Numbers." She has branded herself in her hometown as "The Ritzy Realtor" and is known for her multitude of talents and services. In addition, she is the loving wife to Mr. DeWane Lively and the mother of Kennedy Redwine (12). Santanna grew up on the east side of Detroit where she prided herself on actually making it out. Sadly, many did not. She overcame those environmental barriers that literally folded others. Life for her has been similar to "Survival of the Fittest." She has been blessed with the ability to adapt to any situation without the fear of hindrance. Conquering temptation is one of her greatest skills, as she enjoys leading the way.

Santanna is the principal broker and owner of Ritzy Realty in Detroit, MI. She has also ranked Best Selling Author for her collaboration in "Created For Greatness-Babes n Boots edition". She is a motivational speaker and has spoken on platforms with famous speakers such as Les Brown, Michelle Lovett, Carl Curry, Lateshia Pearson and more.

Santanna landed a lead role in 2023 as "Dallas" in a Murray Production film called "Love All Over Me" where she acted beside Erica Pinkett and was featured in 50 Cents hit series "BMF".

Be on the lookout for her upcoming book "Know Credit" where she educated consumers on how to restore and sustain an excellent credit profile.

It's a Lifestyle

By Geneva McCloud, MPH

I was inspired to start my business in 2014, while working at a Fortune 500 company, I felt unfulfilled and as if I wasn't living up to my full potential. I decided to return to school but wasn't quite sure what to study. I had been to school numerous times and had been unsuccessful in earning a degree. However, this time, I went before God and asked, "What is it you would have me to do?" I heard, *Nutrition*. I took off and earned a Bachelor of Science in Health and Wellness, as well as a Master of Public Health within 4 years through a virtual learning experience.

While studying, I began living what I was learning, and it became a lifestyle for both me and my son. I took control of my own health and managed to lose nearly 40 pounds, reduced my high blood pressure medication, and became a 5k runner. I became affectionately known as Miss Fit in the office and was a part of the Wellness Committee. While on the committee, we started a health hut and were responsible for a monthly newsletter. I fell in love with my new passion for life, and I decided to start an online coaching business.

I'm excited to share with you that I run two women-owned businesses. My first business is Favorable Well-Being, LLC. which has been around since 2016. It is a health and wellness business that focuses primarily on educating people of color on best practices that will create lifetime habits for controlling and managing high blood pressure. I work with a team of service matter experts and collectively we deliver community nutrition and life-changing programs for the youth.

Today, childhood obesity rates are on an upward spiral, causing youth to develop diabetes, hypertension, and high cholesterol before they reach adulthood. The youth nutrition programs offer students a hands-on chef experience in the kitchen using safe recipes that meet a medium-high healthy nutrition score. Nutrition scores are composed of beneficial ingredients and the USDA recommendations for a balanced diet.

My second business started in 2023. Itgigimac is an online nutrition and lifestyle coaching program for Christian women 40 and over with high blood pressure. I share strategies that help guide women to a path of fulfillment and success. During the journey, it may not feel comfortable, but we embrace being uncomfortable to achieve the desires of our hearts.

I feel that what sets me apart from my competitors is that I believe I was called to this assignment by God because of my passion to help others. During my youth, you would find me braiding the hair of little girls on my block and being a help to my younger siblings while my parents worked. I believe my lived and learned experiences have given me a unique approach to explaining the cause of blood pressure and the best methods to reduce and manage it. I trust that when we know the root cause of an illness, we can control it much better. In my study of elevated blood pressure (Public Health Biology Pathophysiology), I learned that potassium controls nerve impulses and a lack of potassium causes anxiety, mental illness, stroke, and cardiovascular disease. As Christian women, we can find ourselves overwhelmed, consumed, and not getting any peace. We are often anxious or worried, but according to the word of God, we are to be anxious for nothing (Philippians 4:6-7). *Be careful for nothing: but in everything by prayer and supplication with thanksgiving let your request be made known unto God. And the peace of God, which passeth all understanding, shall keep your hearts and minds through Christ Jesus.*

In my coaching program, there is a 1:1 Coaching Plan where we change how we see food and learn about its healing effects on the body. We must be accountable and treat our bodies like it's our business and no one else's. We dive into minerals, vitamins, and their nutritional values. We explore nutrition facts and labels. Clients are introduced to tools and resources like My Fitness Pal, which helps to create a balanced meal plan focusing on the macronutrient mix for energy in and out. We set goals and achievable timelines, with an intentional mindset to overcome risky behaviors and barriers leading to metabolic disease states. Listen, I believe our body is the temple, and should be treated as such, to age gracefully.

Weight loss is typically the goal of every client, but that can't be the only focus, because that only leads to yo-yo dieting. At one point in time, I was on that rollercoaster of a diet, and as a result, lost my gallbladder. I was concerned with how I looked physically not realizing I was destroying my body. We must keep in mind that when we were created, God knew every inch of our being and created each of us in a unique way. With that being said, we know there is no one plan that fits all. Plans were set for our lives before we were born. I realized my body was bought with a price and that I must treat my body like it's my business. Remain mindful of the Spirit of God that dwelleth inside. It's time to position yourself for your victory! It's Go Season!

I have overcome some of my challenges by believing in myself. If you were to look up the meaning of GiGi, you would find that she is a free-spirited girl whose heart desires to make a positive difference in the world. Because of my caring nature, I find myself helping others pursue their dreams and begin to lose focus on my goals and dreams because of the gifts of love that live inside me. I had to learn to focus on myself if I wanted to be successful. I believe those actions were the result of my losing faith in myself. I found myself helping others because things weren't moving as quickly as I thought they should. But it's Godspeed so that we are fully prepared for the blessings that are in store for us. I realized growing, learning, and planning were things that would continue through my entrepreneurial journey and to be patient because this is not a race, but a marathon.

I never would have imagined I would study health science after years of customer service. Starting my business while a student in grad school was a huge challenge for me but having a business mentor was clearly the best thing I could have ever done. It felt it both rewarding and fulfilling to be the new kid on the block in my 40s. One thing I've learned: Being patient is certainly a virtue; all your witty ideas will require steps and you don't want to miss any. But when you do, chalk it up to a learning experience or better yet, look at it as if you were an intern -- you get the point. However, one thing to remember is that success doesn't come overnight. It can take years behind the scenes before you are noticed.

Being a business owner takes a lot of guts; each day is different. It's not like going to work for someone else. You experience the good and the bad and will have to overcome many obstacles. The grind is daily and you must start your day with a positive mindset to reach your goals to be successful. So far, 2023 has been mind-blowing. One blessing after the other, and God has shown me so much favor.

But if I had to describe my biggest success, thus far, it would have to be being invited by Visionary Apostle Sabrina McKenzie to share my testimony in this amazing collaboration with other God-fearing Business Women. We have been chosen to do Kingdom Work -- to share steps in overcoming defeat and barriers. We are here to inspire and encourage other women to allow God to order their steps to be a powerful force in the marketplace. Be all-knowing that God will give you the desires of your heart.

Surrendering to the Word of God has made me the woman I am today. I put my life in God's unchanging hands. I had to learn to hear his voice so that I could eagerly respond and obey. But discerning the word of God can be tricky when the enemy is on your trail. The enemy will come disguised in sheep's clothing to kill, steal, and destroy the plans God has for your life if you are not mindful. This year is identified as a year of restoration, and my faith has been restored. I am forever grateful for God's Grace and Mercy over my life, and I trust that I'm going to have just what I want. **"There is a power that is not intimidated by my circumstance." (Bishop Garner)**

I am motivated by the word of God. I heard him say, "Arise GiGi, virtuous woman.

(Proverbs 31:20-21). "Listen to the Word of God, the God that lives inside." I realized it was time to follow the assignment and allow God to take the wheel and be the worldwide navigator to my destiny. He said, "Your health and wealth depend on it. Your family is depending on you. The assignment is important and must not be compromised." I continued to pray and meditate on the Word of God daily and received wisdom and understanding. He went on to say, "Continue to be in fellowship with others who seek the kingdom." I obeyed without resistance. I now know that God's plan is to prosper me and will cause me no harm or danger; I will weather the storm. I know where my help comes from and can now see endless possibilities.

As a wellness professional and businesswoman, I am diligent in creating goals that are specific, measurable, achievable, relevant, and timely (S.M.A.R.T.). SMART Goals can lead to success when you know what it is you want to accomplish and why this is important to you. I must also say that without the encouragement of my son, I would not have taken this leap of faith.

Within the next 5-10 years, I see myself planning an annual wellness retreat for Christian women. The retreat will be a place of love and caring where women can come together and feel liberated. This will be a place of sisterhood and fellowship where women will uplift and inspire one another to make healthy living a lifestyle. You can also look for merchandise on itsgigimac.com and a book release. I see myself making a positive difference in the world, continuing to advocate for democracy in public health issues.

Staying knowledgeable about the latest trends and innovations is key. One thing being a business owner has taught me is to make the vision clear. I make sure my customers know who I am, what I do, and why I care. I know change is inevitable, therefore, ongoing professional training is a must to ensure I am continuously knowledgeable of my customers' needs. The use of digital design tools, such as Canva, Fiverr, and Upwork have been game changers.

My business is shaped by integrity, inclusion, teamwork, and customer commitment. We operate with sound judgment, good morals, and values. We pride ourselves in creating a culture of always doing the right thing at all times which helps to maintain relationships and partnerships built from honesty. Over the years, I have established some trusted bonds and partnerships to bring health and wellness to the communities we serve because of a shared vision. Through our collective efforts, we can protect, promote, and improve the health of our communities.

I stand by diversity and inclusion, seeing that my business is a minority-owned business. I certainly could not see it any other way. When I talk about teamwork, this can include clients, employees, contractors, vendors, volunteers, business owners, and many others. No one is exempt. When the team is driven, dedicated, motivated, and aspires to make an impact in this world, we are unstoppable. "Iron sharpens iron" and I believe in the adage, "Teamwork makes the dream work!"

Measuring success is helpful in your business and lets you know where you stand at all times. Success can be measured in several ways. When strategizing, creating a timeline keeps me accountable and on schedule. Another critical component of metrics includes customer satisfaction. Knowing my customers' likes and dislikes of a process gives me an idea of what's working well.

A skilled marketing and sales executive is highly recommended for measuring the success of your company. The talented person can evaluate analytics and tracking from not only your website, but other search engines including Google, Twitter, and Facebook. They can improve rankings on search engines and convert potential leads back to their prospective carts by recapturing missed sales opportunities.

Connect with Geneva "GiGi" McCloud, MPH

www.favorablewell-being.com

www.itsgigimac.com

genevamccloud@gmail.com

itsgigimac (IG)

Geneva GiGi McCloud (Facebook)

Meet Geneva GiGi McCloud, MPH, BSHW

Geneva GiGi McCloud is a child of God and a Detroit, MI native. She is a mother, caregiver, entrepreneur, and lifestyle coach. She enjoys running 5K races and spending time with her family. In 2014, she discovered her purpose and passion and returned to school, studying nutrition which prompted her to take control of her health. It has been nearly 10 years since Geneva founded Favorable Well-Being, established with the sole purpose of coaching women 40 and over to manage and control blood pressure.

Geneva has served on non-profit boards and committees for nearly 20 years, committed to reducing chronic illness, homelessness, and domestic abuse. In 2023, she was recognized as a Detroit Boss and received The LEEC Award, and was named Chef when her pecan chicken salad recipe was featured in the Partnership for Food Safety Education 25th Anniversary Cookbook.

She is driven by her strong faith in God (Hebrew 11:6). In Him she finds her strength and wisdom. Geneva is planning a women's wellness retreat and looks to expand her business globally. More to come!

Bizzie as a Bee for My Legacy

By Breanna Buchanan

Growing up, my mother worked a lot of double shifts being a certified nursing assistant and as the oldest, she trained me first on all of the ways to maintain a household. Although it drove me mad as a teenager, once I became an adult, now having my own children, those skills gave me the freedom to do both with no pressure. I started cleaning when I was 17 and just needed some cash to put gas into my first car. My mentor was asking me to keep an eye on her residents via her home healthcare business, and I would clean while I was there. The families were so impressed, they sent me to cousins and aunts and before you knew it, I had a client for every day of the week.

Bizzie Bees Experience LLC is all about the customer service aspect, as well as ensuring all of the client's needs are met. At the moment, I am working on creating an environment-safe degreaser and wall cleaner that I would like to sell, and with my work ethic, I'm sure I'll accomplish it. I offer home cleaning, as well as cleaning for small businesses. Surface and detailed cleaning are my main attractions and as stated, building a comfortable relationship with the client and their family to make sure they receive every task they request is a must.

My business differs because I believe in being on a personal level with clients to create a relationship of trust to ensure that I fully and accurately understand their request for the services needed. I believe that interacting with the client ensures an understanding of how they would most like you to operate in and around their homes. I am different from other cleaning companies because of the personal attention I give to each and every client. I give my clients personal one-on-one time with me and no matter the request, I execute them at all costs.

The biggest challenge of my company occurred this year, and it was when I lost my car due to an engine oil leak. It made it hard to get to the jobs, but I will never give up when I'm needed by so many people. I've learned that the type of business I run is a customer service establishment where excuses can't live because of the need-to-want ratio. Also as stated before, my clients are more like associates because of the rapport I build with them in such a personal experience. In spite of this challenge, I made sure to take care of my clients without excuses.

My biggest achievement in this company has been the ability to be available for my children whenever they need me and to not miss out on experiences, mishaps, or just time with them because I schedule my hours to accommodate my family's needs. I believe that all of the hard work and dedication I put into my work and the push I give myself is all I need to feel like a superhero for my community, elders, moms, dads, associates, and others. My customers know that the task will not only be completed quickly but efficiently. I believe in quality, and for that reason, I believe and know in my heart I will be able to pass that business ethic on to my children once they are of age to carry on the legacy.

I stay motivated and focused on my goals because I am a planner. I believe in confirming appointments at least two days ahead of time to avoid any small changes that could alter our appointment. I ensure that I do not miss out on the experience of my getting to know them and providing the best reassuring and relaxing conversations while also the best cleaning service they have ever experienced. I don't just clean but I build relationships to create a safe space for my clients to get all their desires met in their cleaning sessions. I believe that trust and honesty go a long way when ensuring all tasks are completed and I don't mind if during our conversation they feel comfortable sharing something that's been bothering them as well. I am a good listener.

The vision for Bizzie Bee is to have multiple employees and sites in different parts of the world; to cater to and assure that no matter the task, it can be handled by a Bizzie Bee. In five years, I will have expanded across the Midwest and won't just be cleaning homes but will never forget where I started. I love my introspection into my clients' lives and completing their requested tasks. Bizzie Bee will be known by big and small companies for our reputation of satisfaction and assurance. In ten years, I would like to be able to continue to employ the youth and give them avenues for starting their own businesses and endeavors to constantly break generational curses until they no longer exist! The goal is unity like a beehive where we all flow in a way that changes the work dynamic, as well as the field of cleaning. I would like to even advance into crime scene cleaning to employ those who enjoy the criminal justice field. The goals are everlasting, growing every day, and nothing can stop the goals and plans set up for the Bees of Bizzie Bees Experience, LLC!

I am delving into innovation by keeping our social media current with the results of the great work we are doing with before and after photos and recordings. I plan to employ one staff member to record our cleaning process and to share with others the knowledge of how to properly handle different types of stains, proper cleaning of stoves, cabinets, etc.

Some of my main values are trust and discernment. You have to build a strong, trustful bond to be allowed into people's homes and for them to feel comfortable. Being genuine is also another key factor to being a part of Bizzie Bee. People love when you can relate to them and their situation and know that they aren't being judged for the job you're being paid to do. I believe in caring for the needs of clients and assuring that you understand and effectively listen so that your work is a clear response to their needs. Being in the field of customer service, you have to know how to accept criticism as well as be accountable for all of your actions, and that is one of the many things I believe make my company interesting and different.

Our success is measured by return customers and referrals. Most of my clientele comes from word-of-mouth and referrals of satisfaction. I listen and attack the task as if I were a bee obtaining honey for the hive. Error isn't inevitable but we use our time wisely. The more recurring clients I have, the more I know that my bees and I are clearly setting the bar high for a start-up company and there's not anywhere we're going from here but up!

Bizzie as a Bee for My Legacy

Breanna Buchanan

Connect with Breanna Buchanan

Instagram is Bizziebeesexperiencellc

Bizzie Bees Experience LLC Detroit, MI 48211

(313) 544-6393

Meet Breanna Buchanan

Breanna Buchanan is the owner and Queen Bee of Bizzie Bees Experience, LLC. Being a mother of four and coming from a family of five, cleaning has always been a top priority of Breanna's. Although she didn't like it much as a child, the love, support, and clientele that she's established in just two short years is amazing. She cleans homes and small businesses and aspires to one day, service larger venues.

One of the main objectives of Bizzie Bees is to expand the horizon and skills available to people in need. The future of Bizzie Bees will be just as big as Dazzling or Molly Maid Services, but with a repertoire that will explode your mind. She loves people and she loves to clean and with that mindset, she knows she will advance beyond any dreams she has ever imagined.

Mompreneur Making Passive Income with E-commerce

By Shanell Desaussure-Basley, MBA

I have always had the desire to start a business of some sort since about the age of seven. My mom used to say, "Why do you make the kids in the neighborhood play store with you all the time?" I loved cash registers and collecting money as a kid and being in charge of operations. I guess it was meant to be.

I started my business because I was angry at my boss at the time in 2018. It was time for me to return to work after having my first child, and I ran into babysitting issues and notified them in advance to push my return date to the following day. She told me I must report on my return date. I was frustrated and all I knew was that my mouth said, "I will not be returning to work EVER!" I took my savings and maternity leave money and started buying equipment to start making wine glasses and custom t-shirts out of my apartment. I had no clue what I was doing. I knew I was computer savvy, college-educated, and I had the skillsets of a fast learner. I knew people loved their names and pictures on EVERYTHING, and I rolled with that. Belle's Beautiful Creations was born. The name change occurred in 2021 after growth and redirecting a few changes and finding the world of E-commerce and then Blinged By Belle began online.

My second e-commerce business, Stuck Up Girl Collection, started in 2020 with my cousin Felica Simmons as I began to research the life of e-commerce. She assists me at local popup events. I wanted a store that ran on its own and got into dropshipping and ended up creating a combination website of branded items and items I never had to touch or see. It was a new world for me, and I loved it.

Blinged By Belle is a personalization jewelry company. Blinged By Belle jewelry is meaningful, handmade, and tells a story leaving lasting memories. Our top-selling items are our photo memory pendants and our personalized nameplates.

My second business, Stuck Up Girl Collection, is home to trendy items; we are known for our magnetic lashes, press-on nails, and accessories. Stuck Up Girl Collection is available at various local pop-up events and fairs in Detroit, MI. We love having items for our community and customers and most of all we love servicing and communicating with them at the events.

Blinged By Belle is a unique structure because it caters to the customer. Growing up, I'm sure a lot of people, especially urban ladies, could never go to a gift shop or store and find their names. Hello!?!? I was one of them and I hated it. So creating something like that for people that's meaningful was important and I loved everything about it. During COVID, the picture pendants took off like crazy because I had super-fast return times compared to larger companies that were overseas and I personally made them. People's loved ones were passing away left and right and people wanted lasting quality pendants that don't tarnish, fade, or put a dent in their pocketbooks. Blinged By Belle provides that service.

Some of the first challenges I faced when Blinged By Belle started, were during COVID.

Reaching customers and marketing the products was easy but hard. It was easy to market to people in Detroit, but it was during COVID and people didn't want to be near anyone let alone pull up to someone's house or parking lot. I was solely an e-commerce business. People wanted to see the quality. I had to literally post tons of pictures and videos for clients and sometimes, that was still not enough but we overcame by relying on referrals and reviews from satisfied customers.

My biggest success for Blinged By Belle thus far is consistent awareness of the meaningful items we carry, along with focusing on growing, scaling up, and bringing in new Items. Blinged By Belle as passive income for me brings in an additional $25K a year, and I am very proud to say that. It may seem small to some, but I am also still a full-time employee, wife, mom, and daughter. That is a nice side hustle if you ask me. But I want to be a bigger brand in the future and that's what I plan to do with the company, continue to scale it and bring in more revenue.

It gets tough at times to stay focused on your goals; I love meditation (Breathwork), love writing in my gratitude journal, sleeping when I can, lots of therapy and GOD! GOD DID IT I am just following his lead. I used to drive myself CRAZY with my anxiety and depression. It really got bad after my first child. But all the things I mentioned really helped me to see it through. When it doesn't, then time off from everything to reset and get focused helps as well.

My vision for Blinged By Belle is to become a 6-figure business. I plan on teaching peoplethe power of e-commerce and how to start and grow an online business. I want to give back to the community. Show them different ways to earn income besides the traditional 9 to 5. I get a ton of questions so I know that God is leading me in the direction of teaching. I plan to venture off into other passive income also. I love the idea of working for myself and creating my own schedule. Don't get me wrong, entrepreneurship is a tough job but it's far more rewarding when you achieve and accomplish your goals.

Innovation and creativity in my business play a huge part in e-commerce, especially Blinged By Belle. Meeting customer needs and staying attuned to customer feedback and market trends. Embracing change and adaptability in today's changing business, innovation, and creativity are essential for adapting to new technologies, market dynamics, and customer expectations.

Some Core values in my decision-making process are transparency, accountability, privacy, and security of our client's orders, along with fairness and equality. These are all important for my business and growth. These values guide decision-making by setting the framework for responsible and ethical business practices and living life in general.

Measuring success in my business is honestly still a struggle because I feel I'm successful now with way more room to grow. But the e-commerce brand website I use is Shopify. It keeps up with my metrics and shows me my growth and down days. I have an MBA, but I am already a one-woman-show so to see my numbers broken down for me is a great tool the platform offers.

Mompreneur Making Passive Income with E-commerce

Shanell Desaussure-Basley, MBA

Connect with Shanell Desaussure-Basley MBA

833-622-8122 business phone number

Ig @BlingedbyBelle

Facebook @BlingedbyBelle

http://www.blingedbybelle.com

Email address info@blingedbybelle.com

Meet Shanell Desaussure-Basley, MBA

Shanell Desaussure-Basley is the proud owner of two businesses: Blinged By Belle and Stuck Up Girl Collection. Blinged By Belle is a personalized crafted jewelry and special occasion online store. Stuck Up Girl Collection is the home of magnetic lashes, press-on nails, and high-quality fashion accessories.

A proud millennial who graduated from one of the most prestigious high schools in Detroit -- Cass Technical High School Class of 2005 – she believes in empowering and growing yourself as a woman, which is why she is a proud college graduate from Eastern Michigan University earning a bachelor's degree in communications and she attended the University of Phoenix, earning an M.B.A. by the age of 27. She is happily married to D'Aimieon Basley Sr. with two handsome smart boys. She also has a full-time career as a case worker for the State of Michigan. She is beyond blessed and grateful for every opportunity and growing pains she encounters.

Wealth and Wellness is the Real Bag

By Almetia 'MIMI' Thomas

I was inspired to start my business after some years of struggle. Overcoming the stigma and obstacles of being a teen mom has always been my biggest driving force. I didn't want to be another statistic and if I didn't pick myself up, who else was going to do it? I wanted a way out of poverty and violence, a chance to meet my full potential and give my sons all of the love and opportunities I dreamed of. I admit there were days when it felt like nothing was working and nothing was enough. There were good days but there were also days when only my boys ate and nights when I cried all alone. Either way, I'd thank God for the journey and pray for a better destination. Honestly, I know it was my prayers and God that kept me. I started by shutting out the noise and believing in myself and the vision I had for my life.

My business is about promoting the improvement of people's overall health and wellness, as well as promoting the use of all-natural skin care products for their daily skin routine. There are so many unsafe and cancer-causing substances we ingest and constantly put on our bodies. My dream is to teach myself and others how to heal and rebuild their bodies better naturally. I provide a variety of natural skin care products that I hand-make myself. I travel to Nigeria twice a year and while I'm there, I visit the mainland to purchase ingredients to make my products.

I created the spa with the goal of providing a wellness haven for individuals seeking a rejuvenating experience. Misonatural Beauty & Wellness Mobile Spa offers a unique spa experience with a relaxed design and modern amenities. Most clients describe its atmosphere as calming and very tranquil. The massage services at Misonatural are said to be like no other, incorporating techniques such as wood therapy, hot stone, and lymphatic drainage massage to provide a thorough and rejuvenating experience that gets deep into what your body needs. The spa also offers a variety of other services including body scrubs, facials, yoni steams, and foot reflexology.

What makes my business unique is the 100% all-natural products. I literally give you a piece of me because I'm with you from the beginning until you've achieved your goals. I constantly fly to Africa, bringing back the best herbs and freshest ingredients to put in my products. I then put 1000% of my passion into every product or service because I believe in going above the customer's expectations every time. It makes people want to come back and learn and grow with you. Given my nursing background, I make sure each patient is evaluated and given care specific to their needs. I don't have any cookie-cutter recommendations or a "one service fixes all," solution to people's problems. We map out realistic and attainable goals to optimize your chances of making changes and sticking to them because consistency is what's key to seeing any true changes.

Some challenges of being a successful Black business owner, which is a real challenge within itself is believing in your vision when nobody else can see it or believe it. it's investing countless amounts of money with possibly no return! Early mornings, with sleepless nights trying to essentially get people to believe in your products or services as much as you do. I've made products I poured my heart and soul into that no one would buy. On the other hand, I've accidentally made products that I was so unsatisfied with but people loved. It's honestly all a big risk that you choose to take on yourself. It could be easy, it could be awful, it could be an instant success, or take years to properly launch and market yourself. But I believe the biggest loss you're at risk of taking is the chance you don't take at all.

My biggest success besides my personal growth and providing better opportunities for my sons is my Mobile Wellness Spa! Man, honestly I'm still floating on cloud 9 like it's still my Grand Opening Day. So, I have to admit, I'm a spa junkie. If I could spend about 50% or more of my free time at the spa, I absolutely would. I even built a wellness room in my house where I make my products and service my clients. I had clients that were driving for over an hour and would keep asking when I would do mobile services. I kept thinking about what that would entail, which would be me cramming all of my equipment in and out of my car which wasn't an option because while God blessed me in so many other areas, we're still working on organization. I'm way better now but in the beginning, the struggle was real! I needed a more efficient way to carry ALL of my products and equipment so that I could service a variety of patients in one day. I was looking for a space and couldn't find anything that fit me. It motivated me to go mobile!

To stay motivated and focused... Whew! I pray, and do vision boards to help me brainstorm, journal, and set obtainable short-term goals that ultimately help me obtain my long-term goals. I make sure to celebrate my small victories like they're big ones! But it's still a combination of things that keeps me motivated and focused. God first and foremost. He's doing most of the work. Honestly, I'm just a vessel. He blessed me with the opportunity to escape the darkness and begin to live instead of simply existing or surviving. So that's most of my motivation within itself. I honestly don't know what I'd do without the power, mercy, and grace of God's love. It's His love and light that keeps me at peace, even on my craziest days. My kids also push me to be the best because I know they're watching. Working with youth and seeing them make changes and thrive feeds my soul. And last but never least my circle keeps me grounded. They encourage me when I'm down, make sure I eat, and make time for self-love and self-care.

In the next 5 years, I envision my brand being a national and international sensation, helping people around the world learn how to love and care for their bodies inside and out! I'll also be getting more involved with the youth both at home, in the US, and in Africa. I've already spoken at several high schools near my home in Jonesboro, GA, and in Detroit, as well as participated on church panels and have helped quite a few less fortunate families during the holidays. But I'd like to actually start a program that would help young mothers get on their feet and give them a chance to be my mentees and become entrepreneurs by running their own Mobile Spa! In 10 years, I'm also envisioning having launched my scholarship program for children (both home and abroad) interested in healthcare or in joining the health and wellness community, essentially bridging the gap between the women in America and the women in Africa.

Innovation is everything in this business, so I'm always looking for new ways to heal and revitalize our bodies. Be it new massage techniques, herbs, equipment, or services. I'm always in seminars, taking classes, or constantly doing research. When you're truly doing what you love and investing in yourself and your craft, staying up to date is rarely an issue! I mean how can it be? If you're fully immersed in your craft, nobody can tell you a thing! And as far as trends, I don't chase those, I set them. And that's simply by doing what I said before, devoting time and money to being the absolute best you can be.

The core values that guide my business and every decision in my life always incorporates the Word of God and doing His work. Using my income to make an impact on my community is what it's all about. I treat everyone with the utmost respect. It doesn't matter if they're worth a million dollars or zero dollars, I treat everyone how I'd like to be treated. I look to teach my people, especially the youth, how to live open, healthy, and unapologetic lives and that there is still hope even when it seems like they're being buried. Remember, it's all in helping people change their mindset. In the words of my good friend Ashley Calderon, "They have to do what they've never done to get what they've never had… sacrifices and all." I want to help them see that they're not being buried, they're being planted! It takes time to bloom, and every flower requires different seasons and conditions. Supporting and strengthening the youth is how we ensure a brighter, healthier future.

When thinking of measuring success, I'd have to say that success for me is relative. I celebrate having a great quarter fiscally like I celebrate a client losing 10 lbs. A win is a win and they're both huge successes in their own right. Of course, if I wanted to quantify it, I'm in the green and we're barely halfway through the year. My business is actually starting to gain solid momentum nationally; my conferences have been bringing in record crowds and being able to network with some of the most amazing and prominent figures has opened doors and had my name in rooms I've never been in. These are some of my biggest successes on paper to date! But the feeling I get when someone doesn't have to use certain medications anymore when someone's stubborn acne clears or that twinkle of inspiration those young girls get in their eyes when they hear my story… is priceless. That for me is true success.

WEALTH & WELNESS
Is The Real Bag

"Wealth and wellness defined."

MIMI THOMAS

- **Connect with Almetia "Mimi" Thomas Beauty & Wellness Expert 678-665-3818 misonatural.com**
- **IG: misonatural_**
- **FB: misonatural mimithomas.net@yahoo.com**

Meet Almetia 'MIMI' Thomas

Almetia 'MIMI' Thomas is a Beauty & Wellness Expert. Serial Entrepreneur, Author, Speaker, and Philanthropist. Founder and CEO of MISONATURAL Beauty & Wellness Mobile Spa and Journey to Wealth Empowerment. She took a leap of faith and moved to Atlanta with her two sons at 22 years of age with no family and no support -- just faith and a goal to break generational curses being the first to become an entrepreneur in the family. In the next 5 years, she desires her brand will be a national and international sensation, helping people around the world learn how to love and care for their bodies inside and out! She'll also be getting more involved with the youth both at home, in the US, and in Africa.

Hype Vibes Recreational Self Care

By Aisha Griffin

I was inspired to start my business after attending my girlfriend's kid's birthday party and the entertainer was frustrated and could not hold the children's attention. The entertainer told me her pay was a hundred dollars an hour. I was a young loan officer at the time and made good money. I enjoyed spending a lot of time with my young cousins, and it was easy and fun for me to keep them entertained. I then began practicing after purchasing twisty balloons, an air pump, face paint, brushes, books, and supplies. I thought my aunt was crazy for asking me to help pay $250 for my cousin's, aka Godson's, clown entertainment at his 5-year-old birthday party. I was determined to perform myself and found some overalls Billy-bob teeth, boom box, dance routines, and games to play.

I remember my mom sucking her teeth, even after I had received multiple bookings from parents to entertain at their next event, and saying that when I was done, I could help them with a mortgage. She did not approve of the idea of her professional loan officer daughter entertaining for children's events, even if I thought it was just going to be a hobby or side gig. Funny enough, today she is my biggest cheerleader, supporting me to accept bigger and better opportunities.

My business is all about offering motivational and keynote speeches, workshops, parties, and engagements for individuals and any group size or age, the seven pillars of self-care services. The products I offer are items used to foster customized plans.

My business is unique because I want everyone that meets me to feel encouraged and better about themselves. I have experienced the need for every aspect of the seven pillars and have researched and tried the before, during, and after effects. I am set apart from my competitors as a passionate Afro-Carib woman that cares about impacting the lives of my clients forever by helping them to continue believing they are the winners forever.

Some of the challenges I face are procrastination, frustration, impatience, overthinking, lack of focus, support, trust, poor organization, time management, and having too many ideas to implement just one. If I am not well, I do not have anyone that can be me. To overcome these challenges, I:

- Practice being patient with myself
- Practice mindful thinking - every action is a win
- Seek, ask, and take assistance
- Declare and decree how God showed how the outcome

- Study scripture on a subject
- Apply better nutrition and rest practices

The biggest success I have had so far is having guests that have attended my events tell me how I lightened their mood by them participating in fun-filled, high-energy, and action-packed activities and experiencing my caring, personable, and humorous personality. This success has developed me into a well-renowned emcee and host for sports, corporate, celebrity events, award shows, radio, and TV News stations for over 30 years. I would have to say this was achieved by accepting bookings I didn't necessarily think I was qualified for but accepting God's call on my life to believe a merry heart does good, like medicine, because there are enough broken spirits in the world.

I am motivated and focused through these methods:

1. Pray, praise, and worship God.
2. Have conversations with my mother and then my three sisters in Christ.
3. Listen, and watch sermons and motivational speakers.
4. Research online businesses, individuals that are similar, and where I strive to achieve.
5. Write down key points and outlines then practice.
6. Focus on gratitude.

My vision for the future of my business is to have a team alongside me instead of being a one-woman show to accomplish the goal of becoming a global motivational, keynote, and guest speaker source for events as well as becoming a top-selling author and having a product line. I see myself impacting the lives of millions for the better with the gifts the Lord has spared my life to share.

To stay up to date with the latest trends and developments, I spend a lot of time researching online successful businesses that model and align with my vision and purpose.

Some of my core values are putting God first, clients second, and money third. As an Afro-Carib female, I strive to carry on my Prophetess grandmother's spirit of caring for everyone and my mother's giving spirit through everything I do in life and business.

To measure the success of my business, I plan on seeking and utilizing a metric evaluating expert company or software to manage the performance and progress of my business.

Connect with Aisha R. Griffin

Recreational Self Care
Influencer Enthusiast Advocate
iHypeVibes
770 318-3652
iHypeVibes.com
ihypevibes@gmail.com

Meet Aisha Griffin

Aisha Griffin is a Daughter of The King, a Prophetess, a Grandmother, a Selfless Nurse Mother, a Mother, and most of all, a Woman of the Lord. Her mandate is to share positive thoughts, speech, and actions versus negative ones until it's second nature. Aisha speaks, writes, and invites those who need a motivational way to balance the overwhelmingness of work and life by taking time to encourage enjoyable life experiences through mental, spiritual, physical, and emotional actions. Her one-on-one and/or custom group activities offer low-key, high-energy, fun-filled, action-packed sessions, outings, and get-togethers. Her biggest aspiration for iHypeVibes Recreational Self Care is to be a global resource to help others overcome stressful, overwhelming, and unbalanced lifestyles.

Don't Get Out Hustled

By Precious Beal

I was inspired to start my own business because I wanted to create a better life for me and my family. I wanted my children to experience a better childhood than I had. I just wanted that luxury lifestyle. I wanted to make it out of the hood and really make it – not just look like I made it. I wanted more, and I knew I needed money to do so. I've always been independent and strong-minded, so a 9-to-5 did not work for me. I wanted to be my own boss and build my own legacy. That's what led me to become a hair stylist, which is a talent I have naturally. Being a hairstylist wasn't enough. I was on crutches three times in one year, which motivated me to start my own event planning and party rental business. I wanted to change my environment so that my kids could live in the best neighborhoods and attend the best schools. I had to be able to afford all this, right? So I built myself a business that would create multiple streams of income. This is where it all started with $700. I bought my first linen, tables, chairs, and tent from Auntie Lasalle who had just closed her event business. I did one event, and I've been booked ever since.

Moving forward to 3 years later in 2019, I took my last $5000 in cash and invested in my venue space, which at that time was the only banquet hall in Harper Woods. I opened on March 30, 2019. I was turning the big 30, and I sold tickets for $30 to fund the Grand Opening. That's the beginning of my greatness!!!!!!

My business is about spreading knowledge, building wealth, planning, designing luxury events, and my spiritual journey with God. My business is built on experience. I believe experiences are everything. I work diligently on providing excellent service. I'm a serial entrepreneur. My goal is to learn and teach people who don't know how to create multiple streams of income so they can learn to support their families with abundance. I pray and write daily and put God at the head of everything I do.

What makes my business unique is the experience of luxury. The effort that I put into my business and my dedication is unmatched! My business is a service-based business that provides service to customers and businesses that are in need of event planning, tax preparation, car rental services, real estate investments, business credit, and consulting. All of my services are detailed and designed for the client. They know that if they come to me, I'm going to give them all I have and go over and beyond for them.

Some of the challenges I've faced in my business were opening the year before the pandemic. The pandemic came and took people and businesses out of the game. But God had other plans for me. I survived the COVID-19 epidemic without savings, loans, grants, SBA or PPL funding. Somehow, I missed that wave! God made sure that my business or family didn't miss a beat. I've also had city and state violations and shutdowns. Imagine sowing into your business and being forced to go back home because the city just didn't want you there. But little did they know that I was one of God's favorites!! God gave His vision for this business and once God gives you a yes, there's nothing a soul on this earth can do about it. Because of God, the doors of the Promising Events Banquet Center remained open. I've also been challenged with eviction notices, financial problems, and small claims court suits (that I won!) God favors me! I went through city and social media bashes and survived! Still Standing! Still Going Strong! My biggest challenge is not giving up when you want, not folding, and finding strength that you didn't know you had! Wiping my own tears when I wanted someone else to wipe them; rocking myself to sleep with a wandering mind. Seems like a lot, huh? It is…but anything is possible! I did not fold! I did not give up! Still here! Still standing! Still believing! Still trusting God!

Let's Talk Big Success! Do you want to hear what success really is behind the scenes? Long days, sleepless nights, discouragement, not making a $1 some days, sacrifice, discipline, balance, structure, having a strategy and key to open the doors that no man can close. Success is all about timing; timing is everything. Being with the right people at the right time and doing the right thing. If your timing is off, everything else will be off. You cannot rush success; you will ruin it. BE PATIENT! My success goes like this: doing everything right for yearsssss, and nothing would work out in my favor. It didn't matter how focused and balanced I was. It didn't matter what I did or tried to accomplish, it did not work. That goes back to timing. It wasn't my time. I just pushed through by all means necessary. God was birthing and building me up until it was my golden show time! I started out as a CNA (certified nursing assistant) and licensed cosmetologist, which molded me into who I have become: an accredited, luxury event planner, a landlord, a leader in my community, and a serial entrepreneur. I've run and operated 3 businesses in Harper Woods, Michigan, which is located on the outskirts of East Detroit. My bread and butter is Promising Events Banquet Center. I'm the owner of the former Promiseland Kid Spa and 33 Car Rental. I was voted top venue in Harper Woods in 2022. I've successfully run my first tax office in 2023, opening with a staff of seven employees. I've faced many challenges these last 20 years, but I never gave up and I stayed consistent!

    Motivation, Motivation, Motivation. Waking up knowing you have no choice but to push through by all means necessary. Having two spoiled bratz by the name of Promise & Aj that are depending and rooting for me is my daily push. I know they are watching me. They really look up to me! When I get up, I'm going hard for them! I have people in my circle that don't have it; they know I'm the mover and shaker in the family. My mother, Ms. Ann, is such a great person – so loving and giving with a smile that will brighten up anyone's day.

Knowing my mom has needs to be met financially and her being on disability and a fixed income gives me that extra drive to go harder! I'm her go-to when she needs to make ends meet. It's not a good feeling or sight to watch, especially knowing the sacrifices and fight she had to go through to get us back in her care. I had to do something to fix this! Being a leader comes with a lot of pressure and expectations. Just knowing you have people looking up to you gives me joy and hope. People need to be encouraged by other people that come from the same circumstances and situations as them. It keeps them inspired. Gives them hope and life. This shows us all that God is real and you can come up from any situation.

I'm looking forward to my next chapter. 5 to 10 years from now, I know I'll be a married millionaire. I have goals of becoming one of the world's most inspiring entrepreneurs. I look forward to becoming the next Coach Stormy Wellington; she is so amazing. I'm going to purchase land and properties from Detroit, Atlanta, Texas, California, Africa and so many other places around the world. God says you have not because you ask not. I've already asked God.

To stay up to date with the latest trends and innovation, I'm always working on my business…planning, designing, creating, and seeing what the next big wave is. I'm always investing in myself, taking classes, attending workshops, conferences, seminars, and attending empowerment events. When it comes to event planning, seasons change, and you must change with it. I always offer packages that cater to my client's vision. My favorite thing I did was to create a team that includes my family. I hire inside my circle.

My boyfriend is my caterer, Derek (D-Boy catering); my son, Antoine, is my treat vendor (The Dessert King); my sister, Tiffany, is my 360 Booth Vendor; my brother, Joe, who saves my life on a daily is my DJ (Dj Nasty). My sister, Star, is my make-up artist (Star Artistry); my sister, Jelisa, is my graphic designer (Royal Roses Designs); and my favorite cousin, Carla, does my party rentals. My family is super talented! There's my dream team! I'm continuously networking for my business and the people that are in my life. Our motto is, "WE DO NOT GET OUT HUSTLED "

I have a vision that I stand by with my business and it's to plan and design unforgettable moments that come with a lifetime of experience. My mission is to provide superb experiences using my event planning services, speaking, networking, and consulting businesses. My goal is to share, educate and provide the world with exceptional experiences with my gifts and talents. I'm dedicated to uplifting, inspiring, and motivating people.

Business is about being strategic, straightforward, honest, and reliable. Clients will continue to support you when you make them your number one priority. Going over and beyond to get the job done is my specialty. Your company must have a strong foundation and strategy, a team, resources, and connections. Always put a face to your brand. Write down your goals and get your thoughts out of your mind and make them visual so you can set obtainable goals. Don't get weary if you don't meet your set deadlines, don't get discouraged. Get up, shake it off so you can reset and learn from your mistakes and begin again. Continue to work on your mindset daily. Develop new skills and most of all stay balanced. Whatever you do "DO NOT GET OUT HUSTLED "

Don't Get Out Hustled

Precious Beal

Connect with Precious Beal

586-362-0935

preciousb313@yahoo.com

Instagram -preciousbeal_

Facebook -precious beal

Meet Precious Beal

Precious Beal is a serial entrepreneur. She is a well-known event planner and owner of Promising Events Banquet Center and Beal Tax and Consulting Group. Precious has a partnership with Motor City Tax Pros, 33 Car Rental, LLC, and a real estate investor. She is a native of Detroit, MI. Her goal is to serve and uplift her community with the motto "Do Not Get Out Hustled" while rising and building a family legacy, breaking generational curses, and building generational wealth. She displays ownership and leadership capabilities around the world. Precious enjoys volunteering and employing her family and her community as she understands that charity starts at home.

How To Be a Lazy Entrepreneur

By Cednaia Sutton

I was inspired to start my business in May 2022. I embarked on a journey to establish my own business, driven by a desire to test my abilities in rapid business development and leverage business credit. As I delved into the online realm, I encountered numerous individuals who were excelling in the financial industry, which opened my eyes to a crucial gap that needed to be filled: the lack of representation and education for people like myself. In my community, there is a dearth of knowledge regarding business, business credit, and how these elements can be utilized to achieve success in life. Despite African Americans comprising the highest percentage of consumers, we are not proportionally represented among the wealth holders in our country. This stark disparity motivated me to be a catalyst for change.

What makes my journey unique is that I did not have the privilege of having coaches or mentors in the financial industry. Determined to equip myself with the necessary skills and knowledge, I made the conscious decision to self-educate. Through relentless effort and unwavering dedication, I acquired a comprehensive understanding of the intricacies involved in the world of finance.

My business ventures encompass a diverse range of industries, as I am a serial entrepreneur with multiple enterprises. These include a tax firm called LCBC Tax, Lee Carters Management which holds both businesses of a car rental service, a real estate business, and lastly a boutique called Lee Carters Boutique. Operating as a virtual business center, we offer comprehensive assistance to individuals and businesses alike.

In the realm of taxes, we provide valuable support to individuals facing tax issues and concerns. Our expertise extends beyond tax matters, as we also assist business owners in kickstarting and expanding their enterprises. One of our key services involves the repair of personal credit and the establishment of business credit exclusively using an Employer Identification Number (EIN).

In addition to our tax and credit services, I oversee a car rental management company called Lee Carters Management. Through this venture, we facilitate seamless and efficient car rental experiences for our clients.

Furthermore, I am actively involved in the real estate industry. Our real estate business encompasses various aspects, including the management of Airbnb properties, engaging in fix-and-flip projects, and offering monthly rental accommodations.

Overall, my businesses strive to provide comprehensive solutions and opportunities for individuals and businesses in the realms of taxes, credit, car rentals, and real estate.

Our business is unique because first, our businesses cover a wide range of industries, including taxes, credit repair, car rentals, and real estate. This breadth of services allows us to cater to diverse needs and provide holistic solutions under one virtual business center. By offering a comprehensive suite of services, we save our clients time and effort by eliminating the need to engage multiple providers for their various requirements.

Secondly, we stand out by prioritizing education and empowerment. Recognizing the lack of knowledge and resources in our target communities, we go beyond the surface-level transactions and actively educate our clients. Whether it's teaching individuals about tax strategies, guiding business owners on building credit or providing insights into the intricacies of real estate investments, we empower our clients to make informed decisions and take control of their financial journeys.

Lastly, our commitment to serving underrepresented communities, particularly African Americans, sets us apart from our competitors. We have a deep understanding of the unique challenges faced by these communities and strive to bridge the wealth gap through our services. By addressing the lack of representation and education in the financial industry, we aim to empower individuals and business owners to achieve greater financial success and build generational wealth.

Overall, our businesses' uniqueness lies in our comprehensive service offerings, our dedication to education and empowerment, and our focus on serving underrepresented communities. We aim to be more than just service providers; we strive to be catalysts for change and agents of financial empowerment in the lives of our clients.

As a business owner involved in multiple ventures, I have faced and overcome various challenges. Here are the strategies I employ:

- Balancing multiple businesses: I prioritize time management and delegation, ensuring each business receives proper attention and resources.
- Competition and differentiation: I emphasize unique value propositions, comprehensive services, education, and a focus on underrepresented communities to differentiate from competitors.
- Building trust and credibility: I provide transparent and reliable services, deliver on promises, and garner testimonials and referrals to establish trust.

- Financial management: I employ rigorous planning, monitoring, and engaging professionals to ensure sound financial management.
- Continuous learning and adaptation: I invest in education, stay updated on industry trends, and incorporate new technologies to remain competitive.
- Obtaining mentorship: I seek alternative sources of guidance, leverage online resources, join industry networks, and focus on self-education.

By addressing these challenges proactively and focusing on customer satisfaction, I ensure the success and growth of my businesses.

My greatest achievement thus far has been the remarkable success I experienced in my first year of business, specifically with my tax business. Single-handedly, and without the guidance of a coach or mentor, I managed to generate a six-figure income. This accomplishment was a testament to my determination, self-reliance, and the knowledge I had acquired.

To achieve this significant milestone, I hit the ground running from the start. I leveraged the power of social media to attract customers and showcase the value I could provide. As I helped my clients grow their businesses and navigate their tax-related matters, they became my strongest advocates, referring me to others in need.

Through their word-of-mouth recommendations, I saw a steady influx of new customers, each bringing their own measure of success.

Surpassing my initial goal of $30,000 within just a few months was a monumental triumph for me. Not only did it signify my ability to achieve my financial targets, but it also provided the necessary momentum and revenue to expand and diversify my other businesses.

This accomplishment taught me the power of determination, self-belief, and the value of delivering exceptional service to my clients. It reinforced the importance of cultivating strong relationships with customers and leveraging their satisfaction to drive growth and further success.

Looking back, this milestone represents a turning point in my entrepreneurial journey and serves as a constant reminder of what can be achieved through sheer dedication, strategic marketing, and a commitment to delivering value to customers.

Staying motivated and focused on my goals is crucial in my journey of helping individuals transform their financial situations and break generational curses. To maintain my motivation, I draw inspiration from the impact I can make in people's lives and the opportunity to pave the way for positive change.

The knowledge that every day or every interaction presents a chance to assist and make a difference serves as a powerful motivator for me. By implementing strategies and providing guidance, I can help individuals heal their financial circumstances and pursue their passions. This prospect of empowering others and contributing to their success drives me forward.

Moreover, I find motivation in the role I can play as a leader and an example-setter. Not only do I aspire to be a source of inspiration for my siblings, but I also strive to positively influence the lives of numerous individuals I've connected with through social media. Knowing that I can lead by example and demonstrate that it is possible to pursue one's passions while achieving financial stability fuels my dedication to my goals.

To ensure I stay on track and achieve these objectives, I employ several strategies. First, I maintain a clear vision of my purpose and the impact I aim to create. This clarity helps me stay focused and aligned with my goals, even during challenging times.

Second, I set specific and measurable targets that allow me to track my progress. Breaking down larger goals into smaller, manageable steps helps me stay motivated as I experience a sense of accomplishment with each milestone achieved.

Additionally, I surround myself with a supportive network of like-minded individuals.

Engaging with a community of individuals who share similar aspirations and goals provides encouragement, accountability, and fresh perspectives, which further fuels my motivation.

Lastly, I practice self-care and prioritize personal well-being. Taking breaks, engaging in

activities that bring me joy, and maintaining a healthy work-life balance are essential in sustaining my motivation and focus over the long term.

By combining these strategies, I am able to stay motivated, maintain focus on my goals, and continue making a positive impact in the lives of others, all while breaking generational financial cycles and inspiring others to pursue their passions.

In the coming years, my vision for the future of my business is to expand its reach and establish a presence in each state across the country. My ultimate goal is to be a catalyst for positive change and a resolution to the unique challenges faced by individuals in different states.

To achieve this vision, I will diligently identify the specific needs and gaps within each state's business landscape. By understanding what is lacking and what resources are required, I can tailor my services to address those gaps. This approach will provide individuals with the opportunities and support they need to thrive and prosper, even if they are starting from scratch.

Looking ahead to the next 5 or 10 years, I see myself at the forefront of this growth, leading by expanding my business and making a meaningful impact in numerous communities. As my businesses flourish, I will continue to leverage my knowledge and experiences to guide others on their journeys toward financial success and personal fulfillment.

Furthermore, I envision myself as a prominent figure in the industry, recognized for my commitment to empowering individuals and breaking down barriers that hinder financial progress. I aspire to be a trusted advocate and resource for people across the country, offering guidance, expertise, and opportunities for growth.

Overall, my future vision for my business is to create a widespread network of support and opportunities, reaching individuals in every state and enabling them to achieve their goals and dreams. Through my endeavors, I aim to leave a lasting legacy of empowerment and transformation, fostering prosperity for individuals who, like myself, have risen from humble beginnings.

Innovation and creativity play integral roles in my business, particularly in an industry that experiences constant growth and evolution. To stay ahead and stand out, I prioritize creativity in various aspects of my operations.

One way that I foster creativity is by providing my clients with ongoing education. As I learn and discover new insights and strategies, I ensure that my clients benefit from this knowledge as well. By sharing valuable information, tips, and techniques, I empower my clients to make informed decisions and take control of their financial journeys.

Additionally, I recognize the importance of digital products in today's market. To meet the changing needs and preferences of my customers, I am actively involved in creating a range of digital resources. These include eBooks, workbooks, financial journals, and even a comprehensive course. These offerings not only provide additional value to my clients but also position me as a go-to expert in all things related to credit. By providing these innovative resources, I distinguish myself from the competition and solidify my reputation as a trusted and comprehensive resource.

To stay up to date with the latest trends and developments in my industry, I am committed to continuous learning and professional development. I actively seek out opportunities to expand my knowledge through industry-specific publications, attending conferences, participating in webinars, and engaging with online communities. This allows me to remain informed about emerging trends, evolving best practices, and new strategies that can benefit my clients.

Moreover, I keep a finger on the pulse of the market by staying connected with industry thought leaders, engaging in networking activities, and maintaining an open mindset to new ideas and perspectives. This collaborative approach helps me stay at the forefront of innovation and remain adaptable to the changing needs of my clients.

By embracing innovation and fostering creativity, I ensure that my business stays relevant, adaptable, and capable of meeting the dynamic demands of the industry. This commitment to innovation, combined with a proactive approach to staying informed, allows me to provide the highest level of service and maintain a competitive edge in the market.

At the core of my business are key values that guide every aspect:

- Integrity: Conducting business with honesty, transparency, and ethical practices.
- Empowerment: Equipping clients and employees with knowledge and resources for their financial journeys.
- Customer-centricity: Prioritizing customer needs, delivering personalized solutions, and exceeding expectations.
- Continuous Improvement: Embracing feedback, innovation, and adaptability for growth and relevance.
- Collaboration: Fostering a collaborative environment, valuing diverse perspectives, and teamwork.

These values shape decision-making, build trust, and create a thriving business that positively impacts individuals and communities.

In my business, I measure success by the positive impact I make in people's lives and the achievement of their financial goals.

While financial metrics are important, I also consider customer satisfaction, referrals, and testimonials as indicators of success. I regularly evaluate key performance indicators such as revenue growth, client retention, and the number of individuals empowered through my educational resources. These metrics allow me to track progress, identify areas for improvement, and ensure alignment with my long-term goals.

How To Be a Lazy Entrepreneur

Cednaia Sutton

Connect with Cednaia Sutton

info - Leecartersmanagement.com

Phone- (866) 890-3236

Facebook- Cednaia Sutton

Meet Cednaia Sutton

Cednaia Sutton is a serial entrepreneur, and she is involved in multiple ventures, including tax services, car rentals, and real estate. She provides comprehensive solutions to individuals and businesses, focusing on credit repair, business credit building, and financial empowerment.

One notable achievement is generating six figures in her first year of tax business, solely relying on her knowledge and determination. She has successfully expanded her businesses and established a strong reputation for delivering transparent and reliable services.

Her future goals involve expanding her businesses across multiple states and becoming a solution provider tailored to each state's unique needs.

Self-Care

By Brandy Ali

I was inspired to start my business after attending a conference. The Shift Conference changed my life and motivated me to strive for my dreams. As a caregiver for my grandmother, I needed to receive a shift in my mindset from all of the successful people on the panel. My life shifted. I started my mobile spa on December 12, 2017, and it was the best decision thus far. Before starting my business, I remember getting on my knees praying to God to send me the people I needed to fulfill my really big vision; making my dreams come true is everything. Creating my empire and legacy is very important and the mobile spa service by Brandy Ali began giving massages in 2003 and after graduating with a degree in health sciences and finishing massage training in 2005, I began contracting services to the top spas and parlors around Metro Detroit. After spending years working for others, keeping only a small percentage for myself, I realized I wanted to be my own boss.

While pondering the how and where; I want to share with you why I fell in love with massage therapy in the first place. Years prior, I'd spent time acting as a caretaker for my grandmother, who often experienced pain and discomfort. My grandmother said I was the only one who could make her feel better with my massages. I told her, "Grandma, I am going to create SpaLand and cater it to senior citizens." I saved my money, prayed, and in June of 2021, I obtained my dream mobile home and converted it to a mobile spa worth $50,000 after purchasing it for just over $16,000 in an online auction and I hit the ground rolling.

What sets my business apart is availability. I wanted to create something that was convenient. You can call me any time, and I will be there in an hour. My clientele leads busy lives and can't always get to the massage parlor. It's important for people to understand their bodies and get routine massages – it's the self-care that we all need. With massages, you learn what feels good, what doesn't, and how your muscles react. My growing team of 12 massage therapists will stretch you, work out your muscles, and use pressure points to relieve stress.

In addition to a variety of massages, including deep tissue, hot stone, prenatal, reflexology, and Swedish, SpaLand Mobile Spa also offers facials, manicures, pedicures, and soon, vaginal steaming. Lovers can also book a date night complete with a couple's massage and dinner prepared by a chef.

The spa features a TV and refrigerator, a main room that expands for more space, and a private room in the back. This summer, I plan to introduce a yacht and bring the same experiences to sea. I'm also gearing up to add more SpaLand trucks, with one specifically for senior citizens, and I want to be able to accept insurance. I've always been driven by my passion to help others. Growing up I was determined to beat the odds of an inner city youth and instead become successful while helping others. There is nothing like making people feel better and being able to provide a mobile service is the best way.

My business is all about self-care. We create a package that's customized just for you. SpaLand Mobile Spa was created to not only bring a different 'touch' to the life of massages but to add variety with a unique flair. With an array of services from traditional to natural to holistic services, SpaLand Mobile Spa is your go-to massage therapy service that can meet your body's needs, whether it is pain relief, stress reduction, or relaxation. SpaLand Mobile Spa provides excellent massages to get you back on track. Self-care has been defined as the process of establishing behaviors to ensure holistic well-being of oneself to promote health and actively manage illness when it occurs. Individuals engage in some form of self-care daily with food choices, exercise, sleep, reading, and dental care.

What makes my business unique from others is that it's a 3-in-one food truck, party bus, and mobile spa. What sets me apart from others is that I'm contracted with a bed and breakfast to create events every year, and I cater to senior citizens that receive 50% off all services.

For almost seven years, I have tried to serve as many clients in need as possible in Metro Detroit. A lot of people have been under a lot of stress and they haven't gotten a massage in a while.

One of the challenges I have overcome is being afraid. That was a huge challenge for me. Overcoming fear opened up more ideas, more creations, and more innovations. Pushing through the good and the bad, and watching growth is a bigger statement. Having a challenge helps you grow and learn; that's what business is all about. Overcoming being afraid was a huge fear but now I take risks and make investments.

The other challenges I've been faced with are investing and making sure I make a profit. I overcome my challenges by learning from my previous mistakes. Every year, I sponsor a Mother's Day event that I create for the public and my clients; it consists of live entertainment, food vendors, and chair and table massages.

My biggest success so far is getting discovered nationwide in the local news, newspapers, articles, and magazines. My story got noticed because it's a spa on wheels, the first in Michigan, and the brainchild of a single mom who, when confronted by the pandemic, continued to offer community members self-care services. In 2020 when all of the spas were closed, I was open; it was a scary situation but I kept the faith. All while people were losing loved ones, I'm coming into strangers' doors blessing them with my gifted hands and making them feel better. Knowing I did that was everything to me. Giving back to my community is what I love doing and getting recognized for the work that I do means everything to me. COVID-19 was a death sentence. Many people survived and many people didn't. I was an essential worker on the front lines. At that time, my business was much needed. It was the time to create in the spa world and that's exactly what I did.

My son motivates me to go harder; my strategy is to create what people want. I let my clients create what they want, and I make it happen. The goal is to continue to create daily, write it, and make it plain; create your rules and live by them.

My vision for the future of my business is to multiply in all 50 states, reaching people all over the world, educating people on how important the body needs self-care and how massage is a great health benefit. SpaLand will offer memberships to people monthly, and eventually have a brick-and-mortar location that's open 24 hours, and a top-of-the-line bath house with all treatments from massages to body scrubs. I see myself in 5 years with a fleet of RVs of different styles that can be customized to whatever occasion it might be.

Innovation plays a major role in my business; I created something fun, different, and convenient. We pull up to your front door. Creating a business that transforms into whatever you need it to be is pretty innovative. The 31-foot-long purple and green RV that transforms into multiple businesses -- what's inside is a whole different world — a variety of massages, stone therapy, facials, manicures, and more.

My core values are accountability, community, resilience, inventiveness, and passion.

Achievement and academic excellence are at the center of what we do. Customer service is number one, along with respect, loyalty, being kind, and creating something for everyone.

The best way that I have learned to measure success is by my failure. This may seem like an odd metric, but in all actuality, it is not. I have learned over the years that my failure is one of my best learning tools to get better at what I do. As a lifelong learner, I will continue to grow as an entrepreneur and woman that is after God's heart to serve His people with dignity, grace, and integrity.

Self-Care
Brandy Ali

Connect with Brandy Ali

313-320-1534

Spalandusa.com

SpaLand USA Facebook

SpaLand instagram

97 Winder Detroit Michigan 48201

Mobile spa

Meet Brandy Ali

Brandy Ali is the founder, owner, and CEO of SpaLand Mobile Spa. She is the first person in this industry to create a three-in-one business on wheels; food truck, mobile spa, and party bus. She has been featured on ABC, Fox, and CBS and recognized in the Washington Times.

One of her biggest accomplishments was launching nationwide during Black History Month.

Brandy's biggest motivator is her son and her belief in God. Her motto is, *I don't give up and I won't give up making my dreams come true.* It makes her so happy and she's able to motivate others to never give up on their dreams. You can do it.

Mental Health - Think and Grow Rich

By Tassha Faison

As I reflect upon what inspired me to become a brain health coach, it was actually a coincidence that brought me here. In 1993, I began my life as a soldier. Meanwhile, adversity in the military, including traumatic brain injury (TBI), hit my life. After experiencing disappointment from the church and various treatment processes, I, fortunately, came to Dr. Amen, who not only treated my ailment but also stirred a passion in my heart to start my business as a brain health coach. So while I spent each day of my life on medications, I discovered a fervent desire to delve into the realms of the brain, unravel its mysteries and offer solace to those whose minds bear the weight of afflictions.

I now serve as a brain health coach and deliver interactive training workshops to various organizations and personnel. My latest establishment is Regal Lifestyle Enterprise, where I help people live a new life by providing practical solutions to renew their minds. I provide coaching and facilitation for all on many levels.

To me, being a brain health coach means more than diagnosing and treating neurological conditions. It means being a champion of healing, and an advocate for well-being.

What sets my business apart from my competitors is that, well, not all neurologists undergo brain trauma and experience the boundless powers of the brain that I did. They work hard for their degree and start working as a professional. On the other hand, during my medication period, I encountered a realization, a profound epiphany that ignited the flames of my calling. So my heart became a wellspring of empathy, overflowing with an unwavering commitment to alleviate the suffering of others, to offer them a glimmer of hope amidst the darkness of storms. Moreover, I am a Certified Neuro-encoding Specialist and have studied brain training with the renowned Dr. Daniel Amen.

As a business owner, I have faced numerous challenges that have tested my resolve and determination. One of the most significant obstacles I encountered was the lack of support from others in the industry. It seemed like a cutthroat environment, with people competing fiercely and withholding valuable insights and assistance.

Instead of finding a nurturing community of fellow entrepreneurs, I often felt trapped in the grips of those who offered help but only spoon-fed information that kept me stagnant. They were more interested in maintaining their dominance than fostering growth and collaboration.

Overcoming this challenge required a strong mindset and a refusal to succumb to negativity.

I realized that relying solely on others for support was not the answer. I decided to take matters into my own hands and sought alternative avenues for growth.

First, I focused on self-education and continuous learning. I devoured books, attended workshops, and immersed myself in online courses that provided practical knowledge and strategies for success. By acquiring new skills and expanding my expertise, I gained a sense of empowerment and independence.

Second, I actively sought out mentors and business advisors outside of my immediate circle.

These individuals were not threatened by competition and were genuinely interested in seeing me thrive. Their guidance and insights proved invaluable in navigating the complex business landscape. They challenged me to think critically, encouraged me to explore new possibilities, and held me accountable for my goals.

Additionally, I turned to online communities and networking events to connect with like-minded entrepreneurs who shared my values and aspirations. By surrounding myself with individuals who believed in collaboration rather than cutthroat competition, I found a supportive network that uplifted me and provided a sense of camaraderie.

It wasn't an easy journey, and there were moments when I felt discouraged and isolated.

However, by embracing a growth mindset, taking charge of my own development, and seeking out individuals who genuinely wanted to see me succeed, I was able to overcome the challenges that came with the lack of support and limited mentorship.

Today, I am proud to say that I have not only built a successful business but also cultivated a community of entrepreneurs who lift each other up, share knowledge, and celebrate each other's achievements. My experience has taught me the importance of resilience, resourcefulness, and the power of finding your tribe in the face of adversity.

In my journey as a business owner, I have discovered that staying motivated and focused on my goals is crucial for long-term success. It's not always easy, but I have developed several strategies to maintain my motivation and drive, allowing me to make steady progress toward achieving my objectives. Here are some approaches that have been effective for me:

- Clearly Define and Visualize Goals: I start by clearly defining my goals and creating a vivid vision of what success looks like. I make them specific, measurable, attainable, relevant, and time-bound (SMART). By visualizing the desired outcome, I create a sense of purpose and keep my goals at the forefront of my mind.

- Break Goals into Actionable Steps: I break down my goals into smaller, actionable steps. This approach helps me avoid feeling overwhelmed and allows me to focus on one task at a time. I prioritize these tasks based on their importance and urgency, ensuring that each step brings me closer to my ultimate goal.

- Develop a Routine and Set Deadlines: I establish a daily routine that aligns with my goals. I allocate specific time slots for different activities, including strategic planning, focused work, learning, and self-care. By setting deadlines for each task, I create a sense of urgency and hold myself accountable for completing them.

- Seek Inspiration and Stay Positive: I surround myself with sources of inspiration and positivity. This includes reading books, listening to podcasts, attending motivational events, and connecting with like-minded individuals. Engaging with uplifting content and supportive communities keeps me motivated and reinforces a positive mindset.

- Celebrate Milestones and Progress: It's important to acknowledge and celebrate milestones along the way. By recognizing and rewarding myself for achieving small goals, I stay motivated and build momentum toward larger accomplishments. This positive reinforcement helps me maintain a sense of achievement and progress.

- Embrace Continuous Learning: I believe that learning is essential for personal and professional growth. I dedicate time to acquiring new knowledge, skills, and insights related to my industry and business. This constant learning fuels my motivation and allows me to adapt to changing circumstances and seize new opportunities.

- Practice Self-Care and Maintain Balance: Taking care of my physical and mental well-being is vital for sustained motivation and focus. I prioritize self-care activities such as exercise, meditation, hobbies, and spending time with loved ones. By maintaining a healthy work-life balance, I recharge my energy and remain motivated in pursuit of my goals.
- Adapt and Course Correct: The path to achieving goals is rarely linear, and challenges and setbacks are inevitable. I embrace a flexible mindset and view obstacles as opportunities for growth. If I encounter difficulties or need to adjust my approach, I am open to course correction and adapting my strategies to stay on track.

By implementing these strategies consistently, I have been able to stay motivated and focused on my goals as a business owner. Remember, motivation is not a one-time event; it requires daily effort and commitment. With a clear vision, structured planning, positive reinforcement, continuous learning, and self-care, you can maintain your motivation and make significant progress toward your goals.

What helps me to stay motivated and focused on my goals is having a clear vision for the future of my venture. In the next 5 to 10 years, I see my business flourishing and making a significant impact in its industry. My vision encompasses several key aspects:

- Growth and Expansion: I envision my business growing both in terms of revenue and market reach. By implementing effective strategies and leveraging emerging opportunities, I aim to expand my customer base, penetrate new markets, and establish a strong presence nationally or even internationally.

- Innovation and Adaptability: I believe in the power of innovation and staying ahead of the curve. In the coming years, I see my business embracing new technologies, trends, and customer demands. By continuously evolving and adapting to changing market dynamics, I aim to remain a leader in my industry.

- Exceptional Customer Experience: Customer satisfaction and loyalty are paramount to the success of any business. I envision my company providing an exceptional customer experience, going above and beyond expectations. By understanding and anticipating customer needs, delivering high-quality products/services, and providing personalized support, I aim to cultivate long-lasting relationships with my customers.

- Strong Team and Company Culture: As my business grows, I see myself building a strong team of talented individuals who share my vision and values. I aim to create a positive and inclusive company culture that fosters creativity, collaboration, and continuous learning. By empowering my team members and providing them with growth opportunities, I believe we can achieve remarkable outcomes together.

- Social and Environmental Responsibility: I am committed to making a positive impact on society and the environment. In the next 5 to 10 years, I see my business actively incorporating sustainable practices, reducing its carbon footprint, and supporting social causes aligned with our values. By being a responsible corporate citizen, I aim to contribute to a better world while running a successful business.
- Recognition and Influence: I envision my business gaining recognition as a thought leader and influencer within the industry. Through thought-provoking content, industry collaborations, and speaking engagements, I aspire to contribute to the advancement of my field. I aim to be seen as a trusted authority, sought after for expertise and insights.
- In 5 to 10 years, I see myself leading a thriving business that has achieved significant growth and recognition. I will be surrounded by a dedicated team, passionate about our shared vision. Personally, I envision myself continuing to learn, adapt, and grow as a business leader. I will seize new opportunities, embrace challenges, and remain committed to making a positive impact through my work.

While the future may present unforeseen hurdles and opportunities, I am confident that with perseverance, strategic planning, and a steadfast commitment to my vision, I will be able to realize my goals and propel my business toward greater success in the years to come.

As a lifelong learner, I believe innovation and creativity form the dynamic threads that weave together success and propel businesses into uncharted realms of prosperity. So to stay informed with the latest trends and developments, I have loads of perpetual quests for knowledge and curiosity, and I keep exploring emerging technologies. Moreover, I see no shame in seeking customers' feedback in order to understand their evolving needs, preferences, and pain points. Also, I organize surveys, focus groups, and social listening to gather valuable insights that can fuel innovation and drive business growth.

Within the intricate world of business, the core values that serve as the guiding stars in my business are:

1. Innovation
2. Integrity
3. Empathy
4. Excellence and
5. Collaboration

Equipped with all five wings, I go the extra mile to grasp my customer's mental problems and decide their solutions accordingly. In simple words, I pour individual attention on all my clients and deliver motivation so they can come back to their happy life!

In evaluating the success of my business, I rely on various metrics and factors that align with my vision and goals. While financial indicators certainly play a role, I believe success encompasses broader aspects. Here are the metrics and measures I use to assess performance and progress:

- **Revenue and Profitability**: Financial indicators, such as revenue growth, profit margins, and return on investment, provide insights into the financial health and sustainability of my business. They help gauge the effectiveness of my strategies and the overall value my products or services deliver to customers.

- **Customer Satisfaction and Retention**: I consider customer satisfaction and retention as critical measures of success. Positive feedback, repeat business, and referrals demonstrate that my offerings meet customer expectations and generate loyalty. I collect customer feedback through surveys, reviews, and direct communication to continuously improve and enhance their experience.

- **Market Share and Competitive Positioning**: Monitoring market share and assessing my competitive positioning enables me to gauge the success of my business within the industry. By tracking market trends, analyzing customer preferences, and conducting competitive analysis, I gain insights into how effectively I'm capturing market opportunities and differentiating myself from competitors.

- **Innovation and Adaptability**: I measure success by assessing my ability to innovate and adapt to changing circumstances. This includes tracking the introduction of new products or services, implementing technological advancements, and staying ahead of industry trends. The ability to embrace innovation and adapt to evolving customer needs helps me maintain a competitive edge and drive long-term success.

- **Employee Engagement and Development**: I believe that engaged and motivated employees are crucial to the success of any business. I measure employee satisfaction, retention rates, and engagement levels to gauge the overall health of my workforce. Additionally, I monitor employee development, training initiatives, and advancement opportunities to ensure continuous growth and a positive work culture.

- **Social and Environmental Impact**: Success, to me, goes beyond financial gains. I evaluate the impact of my business on society and the environment. Metrics such as carbon footprint reduction, social responsibility initiatives, and community involvement help me measure the positive contribution my business makes toward sustainability and societal well-being.

- **Personal and Professional Growth**: As a business owner, I also assess my personal and professional growth. This includes reflecting on the knowledge and skills I have acquired, the leadership and decision-making capabilities I have developed, and the impact I have made within the industry. These aspects of growth contribute to my overall sense of success and fulfillment.

By considering these comprehensive metrics, I obtain a holistic view of my business's performance and progress toward my goals. It allows me to gauge not only financial success but also the positive impact I have on customers, employees, the market, and society as a whole. Continuous monitoring, analysis, and adjustments based on these metrics ensure that I am on track to achieving the success I envision for my business.

Mental Health
Think and
Grow Rich

Tassha Faison

Connect with Dr. Tassha Faison

Email: info@yourregallife.com

Website: www.yourregallife.com

Ph# 855-734-2580

Meet Tassha Faison

Tassha Faison is a visionary, author, and educator who intertwines brain health and spiritual transformation.

Through captivating storytelling and actionable techniques, she guides readers on a transformative journey to unlock their mental power. As the former Vice President of Women with a Call International and an instructor of the School of Prophets, and now founder of Regal Lifestyle Enterprise, she impacts lives globally. Certified as a Neuro-Encoding Specialist and a John Maxwell Coach, Tassha connects with clients from all walks of life. With a wealth of knowledge and 20 years of service in the United States Army, she revitalizes individuals and organizations through interactive workshops, aiming to change the world one person at a time.

7 Steps to a 720

By Sabrina McKenzie

It is honestly an honor to journey with you as you increase your credit score to the 720 Club to live a life of financial freedom. The myth is to do a credit sweep and live happily ever after. We all wish it was that easy, however, credit is a journey, not a sprint. The same way you shower every day to stay fresh and clean is the exact same way you need to work on monitoring your credit monthly.

Our company Credit Marketplace Center is designed to help you clear up and maintain good credit.

Here are 7 Steps to a 720 Credit Score; if you need additional help, schedule an appointment and our credit specialist will work with you right away.

I NEED SOME PEOPLE TO WORK FROM HOME

ALL ONLINE AT HOME, RECEIVE DIRECT DEPOSIT OR CHECK & FULL TRAINING PROVIDED.

Pastor Sabrina McKenzie
WOMEN'S RIGHTS ACTIVIST

Step 1. Register and grab your free weekly credit report here: Access your credit reports on all 3
Bureaus: https://www.annualcreditreport.com/index.action

Step 2. Register with our company:
https://www.ucesprotectionplan.com/proplan99.aspx?rid=SMckenzie4

Our Credit Attorney will write letters for all your derogatory items. (Where do they register?)

https://www.ucesprotectionplan.com/proplan99.aspx?rid=SMckenzie4

Step 3. Locate your inquiries and negative Items: Whenever you check your credit report, you'll find a section titled, "Credit Inquiries" or "Regular Inquiries." Inquiries can remain on your report for up to two years and can lower your credit scores.

Step 4. Highlight or circle the specific inquiries you want to have disputed:

Did you know that inquiries can bring down your credit score? Only dispute inquiries that you do not have an open account with. You also have the option to highlight old addresses, employers and inaccurate name spellings as well. (Note: You must highlight any leftover items every cycle you dispute your credit reports.)

Step 5. Email the edited version of your Credit reports to reports@united-credit.org

Step 6. We will send out all your dispute letters once you are signed up with our credit repair program.

If you have not received your paperwork within 15 business days of emailing your credit reports or if you want to receive your dispute letters via email, please call customer support and request the digital copy to download.

Step 7. Your results from all 3 credit bureaus should be mailed back within 40 days after you place them in the mail.

Please email your results to reports@united-credit.org. If you have not received ALL 3 updates back from the bureaus by DAY 50, please get a NEW digital copy from https://www.smartcredit.com/?PID=50248&ADID=5000 ($9.95 - Look For 3B Reports & Scores) and email your results.

Step 8. Contact our administrator at Admin@wealthcircle.us

Regarding tradelines or to walk you through the steps that will increase your credit score by 100-200 points

Make an Appointment and select a time to talk that works best for your schedule.

Deborsh Crump admin@wealthcircle.us